A PLUME BOOK

COMMIT TO WIN

HEIDI REEDER, PHD, is an award-winning professor at Boise State University, where she teaches courses in communication and commitment. She has authored articles for leading social psychology journals and provides keynotes and workshops for professional organizations, including Citi Credit Cards, Bank of the Cascades, and DIRECTV. Visit her at www.HeidiReeder.com.

Praise for *Commit to Win*

"*Commit to Win* is at once readable and rich with ideas, both fun and important. Heidi Reeder reveals the complexities and dispels the myths that surround commitment, and sketches a compelling framework that explains why committing is sometimes so difficult, and how to right the ship when commitment wanes. Well worth reading if you've ever struggled to follow through on a plan that seemed important but somehow fell by the wayside."

—Adam Alter, *New York Times* bestselling author of
*Drunk Tank Pink: And Other Unexpected Forces
That Shape How We Think, Feel, and Behave*

"This book sheds light on a crucial (but often overlooked) question: Why do some people persist with important goals while others do not? A must-read for those interested in the science of achievement."

—Cal Newport, author of *So Good They Can't Ignore You*

"Commit to read this superb book, now! Heidi Reeder will help you reach your goals." —Barbara Morgan, NASA astronaut (ret.)

"What a useful and entertaining book! Heidi Reeder's simple explanation of the four-element formula for commitment can help you into—or out of—a commitment such as a relationship, a workout routine, a job, or a project. A valuable addition to the psychological literature."

—Meg Selig, licensed professional counselor, author of
Changepower! 37 Secrets to Habit Change Success
and the *Changepower* blog at psychologytoday.com

"[*Commit to Win*] is meaningful. Up-to-date. Helpful. It is written in a way that doesn't talk down to you, doesn't talk over your head, and doesn't use anybody's jargon. Reeder engages you right away, and you feel as if the book was written just for you. It was. The last section 'invites' you to develop a plan for one of your own commitment goals and takes you through it step-by-step. It is superbly done. In my opinion this one section alone is worth the price of the book."

—Irene Conlan, MSN, PhD, creator of *The Self Improvement Blog*
and host of *The Self Improvement Show* on VoiceAmerica

"Is [commitment] just a matter of willpower and determination, or is there more to it than that? Dr. Heidi provides the science and the data behind the most pressing commitment quandaries in business, relationships, and life in general."

—Jordan Harbinger, owner of the Art of Charm boot camp and podcast

"Reeder's book offers a detailed look at [the four commitment elements], how they interact to influence our level of commitment to a person, a job, or a cause. She has even produced a mathematical formula to describe this interaction. However, her tone is anything but clinical or obtuse. Instead, she uses easy-to-comprehend and entertaining stories to illustrate the dynamics of commitment."

—*ASU Magazine*

COMMIT TO WIN

How to Harness the
Four Elements of Commitment
to Reach Your Goals

HEIDI REEDER, PhD

A PLUME BOOK

PLUME
Published by the Penguin Group
Penguin Group (USA) LLC
375 Hudson Street
New York, New York 10014

USA | Canada | UK | Ireland | Australia | New Zealand | India | South Africa | China
penguin.com
A Penguin Random House Company

First published in the United States of America by Hudson Street Press, a member of Penguin Group (USA) LLC, 2014
First Plume Printing 2015

 REGISTERED TRADEMARK—MARCA REGISTRADA

THE LIBRARY OF CONGRESS HAS CATALOGED THE HUDSON STREET PRESS EDITION AS FOLLOWS:
Reeder, Heidi.
    Commit to win : how to harness the four elements of commitment to reach your goals / Heidi Reeder, PhD.
        pages cm
    Includes bibliographical references and index.
    ISBN 978-1-59463-133-7 (hc.)
    ISBN 978-0-14-218181-2 (pbk.)
1. Commitment (Psychology) 2. Goal (Psychology) 3. Motivation (Psychology) I. Title.
    BF619.R44 2014
    158.1—dc23   2014001085

Printed in the United States of America
10 9 8 7 6 5 4 3 2 1

Set in Adobe Garamond Pro
Original hardcover design by Eve L. Kirch

CONTENTS

Contents

PART III

ENGAGING THE COMMITMENT EQUATION

INTRODUCTION

Ian was a successful lawyer who defended people in their darkest hour. His clients included people accused of dealing drugs and driving drunk, and a few accused of murder in high-profile cases. Ian was passionate about his occupation. Whenever someone asked how he could defend such "criminals," he explained he was standing up for an important American ideal: No matter who you are or what you've been accused of, everyone deserves a fair trial.

Despite Ian's passion and natural talent for his job, as the years went by he started to feel like he was missing something. Over drinks with friends now and then he'd describe his dream to move to Africa and become a farmer, like his father had been. He mused about purchasing a large tract of land and producing food that would serve the needs of those in Mozambique or Zambia. On other occasions, he would earnestly talk about hosting a radio program, a *He Said, She Said* show delivering practical advice and outrageous antics. But Ian didn't pursue these plans. He continued working for his clients, upholding the value of "innocent until proven guilty." He continued, that is, until one dismal day when he was legally forced to stop. Ian's license to practice law was revoked when a few of his former clients, who were ultimately found guilty, started talking to each other about their legal representation while serving their sentences. They were convinced Ian had dropped the ball during their trial. Despite the evidence against their claims and Ian's vigorous defense, some of the allegations could not be successfully defended. His license was on hold and he was unable to continue his life's work. He went from being passionate about his job—albeit prone to the occasional fantasy of farming in Africa—to being forced out of his career by a few defendants who he believed deserved a fair trial.

Now, some might say losing his license presented a great opportunity. Why not pack the bags and board a plane bound for Africa, or develop a demo for the radio show idea? But Ian didn't do those things. Instead, he has vigorously worked for five years to get his license reinstated so he can practice law. So far, his appeals haven't been successful. He currently teaches social studies to disadvantaged high school students and feels good about the work despite the reduction in personal income. He's confident, though, that he will get his license reinstated, and when that happens, he'll return to the job he loves.

Why did Ian decide to fight for a career he had pondered leaving on so many occasions? Was he simply afraid of the unknowns that come with a new career? Or did losing his license lead him to realize that the courtroom is where he belongs? And what drove him to stay committed to the legal profession despite the bitterness of what had happened and the many setbacks that followed?

We all have meaningful goals, like progressing in a career, supporting a family, or building a dream home. Any goal, regardless of how much it's cherished or how earnestly it's developed, will make little progress unless it is supported by *commitment*. Without commitment, the goals we set for ourselves are mere dreams— ideas that don't have the footing to be realized. Just as motivation provides the energy to set goals and begin the journey, commitment provides the power to stick with it over time so that goals can be actualized. Ian's vision was to get his license back and continue in his ideal occupation. Commitment to that vision sustained him through numerous appeals and setbacks. Without commitment, Ian would have moved on long ago.

I've been studying and teaching commitment for fifteen years. I've learned that what drives commitment is far different than what most of us think—it's more powerful and complex than we often realize. And it's greatly influenced by seemingly inconsequential factors. Ian's story illustrates many principles about how commitment works. First, our goals are often more challenging and take longer to achieve than what we originally thought. Ian never imagined it would take so long to regain his license, and his level of commitment has been essential for him to stay in the fight. Second, we can be unaware of how deeply we value certain parts of our life, and how committed we are to something seemingly obvious, like a career or relationship we may have even imagined leaving. It's when those things are at risk that we realize their importance. Third, our level of commitment to a personal goal can vary significantly depending on key circumstances. We may feel far more devoted one day than we do the next, just as Ian dreamed of becoming a farmer despite his fierce commitment to his clients and his love of the law. We can experience commitment conflict, in which part of us wants to remain dedicated and another part wants to change course. This can be an uncomfortable feeling, and it's easy to think there must be something wrong with us if we're feeling torn about commitment. In actuality, this is how commitment works. It isn't something you just *will* yourself to do. Instead, levels of commitment change, sometimes on a daily basis, depending on the key variables that drive commitment. And here's the exciting news: Some of these variables you can control.

What if you knew how to be more committed to a particular goal in your life? What if you knew the essential steps to *letting go* of something that was limiting your personal growth or something that was no longer right for you? What if you could help other people, like your employees or team members, to be more committed? It turns out you can.

Social scientists have discovered four variables that work together to influence our level of commitment to all kinds of things, from meaningful personal goals to relationships and careers. I call these elements *treasures*, *troubles*, *contributions*, and *choices*. Treasures are what you value about the activity or relationship, the things that make it rewarding to you. Troubles are the downsides of the activity, the costs you incur along the way. Contributions are the personal or financial resources you have already invested—the things you stand to lose if you decide to quit or move on. Choices are other options you may see, and how attractive those options are. The strength of these variables predicts your level of commitment to nearly everything in your life.

When we look at Ian's situation, we can see he treasured certain aspects of his occupation. He loved the law and embraced the justice system, and he didn't mind the comfortable paycheck either. As with all commitments, he experienced troubles. He regularly dealt with difficult people in challenging circumstances, and at times had to endure the stress of losing an important case. Perhaps these troubles led Ian to imagine his other choices, and to fantasize about what it would be like to be on the radio or in Zambia. When it came down to it, though, he discovered he had contributed a large part of himself to his work. He had invested his time, talent, and all his years of training. Even after his license was suspended, Ian continued to contribute significant time and effort in an attempt to get it back. Now he is at a crossroads. He has the opportunity to make a conscious choice about what he wants to commit to. If his goal is to continue the fight in an effort to practice law again, there are steps he can take to strengthen that commitment and go all in. But if it's time to make a change and do something new, there are steps he can take to let go and move on with confidence.

That's where the ideas in this book come in. Part I investigates the importance of commitment in our lives. We rarely consider the power of commitment, even though it drives our long-term decisions and goals. We'll take a fresh look at commitment by separating it from related concepts like motivation and the promises we make to ourselves or others. We'll unveil the pervasive myths about commitment that prevent us from understanding how it really works. The chapters in Part II investigate the four elements that predict commitment—treasures, troubles, contributions, and choices—and how they interact to influence our level of commitment. Part III contains action pages: a comprehensive set of questions and activities to help you identify important goals that will benefit from commitment. The first set of action pages provides a plan for going "all in" and generating increased commitment to a meaningful area of your life. The next set provides steps for moving on and reducing commitment in an area of your life that no longer serves you. The final action plan is for assisting others toward higher levels of commitment.

While I can't tell you what you should be committed to (that's for you to decide), I can tell you how commitment works, and how you can make new choices to develop greater levels of commitment to meaningful goals and reduce your commitment to the things that no longer serve you.

Are you ready? Then let's begin by dispelling the common assumptions about commitment and unveiling some new truths.

· PART I ·

The Power of Commitment

CHAPTER 1

A Fresh Look at Commitment

COMMITMENT is the foundation of all great accomplishments. Without commitment, Amelia Earhart wouldn't have become the first woman to fly solo across the Atlantic Ocean. Without commitment, Bill Gates wouldn't have cofounded Microsoft and become one of the wealthiest people in the world. Without commitment, Roger Federer wouldn't have become the greatest tennis player of all time, continuing to play even after the analysts said he was past his prime. Without commitment, Herbert and Zelmyra Fisher, from James City, North Carolina, would not have been married eighty-six years, garnering the Guinness World Record and a lifetime of love and family. Inspirational stories about commitment are all around, but commitment is also a crucial ingredient for everyday goals, like designing a new marketing plan, training for a triathlon, or even quitting a terrible job so you can move on to something new. Despite its influence, few people truly understand what commitment is or how it's created.

What do you think of when you hear the word *commitment*?

You may instinctively think of a personal relationship or perhaps a professional goal. You may consider commitment a virtue, a vital part of a good and fulfilling life. Or you might associate commitment with being constrained and burdened. Chances are you use the word to mean a variety of things: sometimes as a synonym for promise, vow, or resolution, and other times for determination or hard work. But commitment is a distinct concept, and it's far more complex and powerful than it appears at first glance.

Commitment isn't the same thing as a promise, for example. When the topic of this book comes up, people often say things like, "I know people who totally need to learn about commitment. They tell me they're coming to my jewelry party, and then they don't show up!" In this case the hostess has confused the concept of a promise or a good intention with the concept of commitment. If her friend were *committed* to the jewelry party, it would mean that the friend was invested in it: that she was psychologically attached to attending the gathering and was willing to overcome obstacles to be there. Few people seem to feel that way about jewelry parties, except the hostess and the jeweler.

Commitment also isn't the same thing as motivation. People begin jobs, relationships, health regimens, and creative endeavors all the time. Their motivation to begin is not the same as their willingness to stick with it over time. For example, a woman enrolled in my department's Master of Arts in Communication program because she needed to update her credentials, so that was her initial motivation. Later she found out a master's degree wouldn't help in her career, but she found the program fascinating on a personal level and was already halfway through. Now she was committed to finishing, but for very different reasons than those that prompted her to start.

Commitment isn't always about happiness either. We are certainly more likely to be committed to things that make us happy, but that isn't the whole story. Commitment works to keep you engaged even on troubling days. And it's okay to be committed to things that bring temporary discomfort or frustration. You might not always feel like practicing your musical instrument, for example, but if you've set yourself up to be committed, you pick up your violin anyway.

What Is Commitment?

Commitment is complex, but the main definition from those who study it is this: the experience of being psychologically attached to something and intending to stay with it. That something could be a job, relationship, activity, or personal goal. The Latin origin of the word is a combination of "cum" and "mittere," which translates to "to join, combine, put together." Commitment refers to the degree to which you join and stay, versus the degree to which you separate and go. It's about whether you are looking for ways to make that job, relationship, or activity more meaningful and central to your life, or whether you are trying to break away. We sometimes think of commitment as a thing, but it's better understood as a process. Think of it like a muscle: You don't lift weights one day and then have stronger muscles for life. Muscular strength is a process to develop, and it's also a process to sustain. So it is with commitment. You can develop and strengthen commitment where you need it most.

It's also possible to be quite torn about commitment, to be in the process of figuring out whether to give more effort and stay or to cut your losses and move on. When a job, project, or group no longer adds joy or meaning to your life, it might be time to reconsider your commitments. You can feel guilty about this, immediately assuming that to intentionally lessen your commitment to something makes you weak, or a quitter. But in order to reach your goals, there are projects, people, and environments you'll want to step away from. Sometimes the best thing you can do is *let go* of a commitment and be open to something new.

The Two Sides of Commitment

The reason we use the word *commitment* in many ways, and have both positive and negative associations with it, is because commitments often contain two forces: *dedication* and *constraint*. Dedication is the "want to" part of commitment. It reflects our intrinsic desire to devote ourselves to something we believe is important or meaningful. When you say, "I am really committed to launching my new product line," you are probably thinking of personal dedication. You may be dedicated to your work, your children, or your monthly book club. Your dedication comes from valuing the relationship or activity so much that you are willing to deal with the difficulties and challenges that come with it. Constraint is the "have to" part of commitment. It refers to the restraints that keep you committed, even when you'd rather not be. When you say, "I scheduled to this meeting, so I guess I'd better be there," you are focusing on the constraint side of commitment. You do what you must, because there will be negative outcomes if you don't. Commitments are particularly strong when both forces are present: You are internally dedicated and externally constrained.

Commitment feels negative, however, when it's based solely on constraints. Maybe you're committed to your job, but only because you don't see another option. Maybe you are staying in a relationship, but only because you don't want to divide up your friends after the breakup. Maybe you continue that exercise routine not because it's fun or showing results, but because you bought expensive equipment from the Home Shopping Network. When commitment is based *solely* on constraints, you're likely to feel stuck and have that internal sense you are meant for something else. On the other hand, constraints are quite helpful, and some would say necessary, for long-term commitment, like remaining married.

Commitment is vulnerable when it's based solely on dedication. While constraints are resistant to change, feelings of dedication can vary by the week, or even by the hour. You may feel deeply devoted to your sweetheart one moment, but be ready to walk out at the next difficult fight. You may be totally devoted to your new business plan, until the bank rejects your loan request. Commitment based exclusively on dedication can more easily falter during challenging times. That's why you'll see both dedication and constraint reflected in the commitment predictors discussed in this book.

Commitment Is Innate

In our culture, the way we talk about commitment can make it sound like a highly advanced activity, something that requires great ethics and integrity. But commitment is instinctual. You already have the innate tools to experience high levels of commitment in the key areas of your life. All animals, including humans, are capable of immense devotion. Consider Holly, a four-year-old tortoiseshell-colored cat, who became separated from her loving owners during an RV rally in Florida. Two months after her disappearance, she showed up in her owner's neighborhood and was discovered by a nearby family. Her hind claws were completely worn, the pads of her paws were bleeding, and she had lost half her body weight. It turned out that Holly (an indoor cat) had somehow managed to walk 190 miles home. The family that found her took her to a veterinarian, where the identity of Holly and her owners were revealed in a microchip embedded under her skin. As a result, she was happily reunited with her owners. Scientists are baffled as to how Holly made her way back, but an innate instinct gave her the compass and commitment to find her family.

On the other hand, imagine the fate of a hypothetical baboon who is not committed to the troop. He wanders off and ignores important social gatherings and mutual grooming. He won't remain in the part of the jungle that bears the best fruit. As a result, this baboon will likely struggle, and the same goes for us advanced primates.

The first place we see an instinct for commitment is in children. Groundbreaking studies in the 1960s and 1970s showed that the first commitment—forming a secure attachment to a caregiver as a young child (ages twelve to eighteen months)—has tremendous implications for commitment patterns later in life.

Let's go back to when you were a toddler—that age when you'd learned to walk and to deftly handle your sippy cup. You could get out a few important words like "no" and "baba," but it would be a while before you could master your ABCs. Let's say you're hanging out in a room you've never been in before, just you and your primary caregiver, who we'll call Mama. In this room you are allowed to explore and check out the Nerf balls. How far from Mama will you roam? You might stay right by her side, or you may wander off, unconcerned with her presence. Perhaps you explore just a bit, but you also make sure she's always in sight. Now imagine a funny-smelling stranger enters and starts talking to Mama. After a few moments the stranger turns to greet you, reaching out his giant hand. How do you feel now? Perhaps it's uncomfortable, or perhaps it's okay, as long as Mama is near. Now Mama leaves and so does the stranger, and suddenly you're in this room by yourself. How unsettling is this? You might be unconcerned and oblivious, or you might feel abandoned. Then Mama comes back into the room and comforts you. Are you happy to see her and calmed by her presence? Or are you on the verge of an angry meltdown?

It turns out that how children respond to this series of events, called "A Strange Situation" by child psychologist Mary Ainsworth, tells us a lot about their attitudes toward committed relationships later in life. Most of us want to be what Ainsworth calls *securely attached* to our primary caregiver because, as you'll see, those who are have it a bit easier later on. All of us were committed to a primary caregiver in some manner; it's just a matter of how secure that attachment was.

In Ainsworth's studies, securely attached children felt safe to explore the room as long as their parent was in close proximity. They were friendly with the stranger when their caretaker was present, but avoided the stranger when she was out of the room. They were distressed when their parent was gone, but immediately went to her for comfort when she returned. This pattern pointed to a solid or "secure" base for the child. Those with secure attachments in childhood are more likely to believe as adults that love endures (hello, commitment!), have higher self-esteem and a greater ability to connect socially, and develop close and trusting relationships.

Some children showed what is called an *avoidant* attachment style.* These children avoided or ignored their caregiver, and didn't seem to react one way or another when she came and went. They tended to be disengaged not only from their caregiver but also from their environment and from other people. As these children grow up, they are more likely than others to see love as temporary. As adults, they tend to avoid investing in both social and romantic relationships, and they engage in more casual, non-intimate sex.

Other children were characterized as having an *anxious* attachment style. These children were tentative in their environment and were likely to keep their distance from strangers, even in the presence of Mama. They were typically highly distressed when Mama left, but ambivalent when she returned. These children are more likely to grow into adults who form relationships reluctantly and then behave in jealous and clingy ways when they worry their partners don't love them. As you'll see in Chapter 6, some of the patterns of attachment style show up in the workplace as well.

When psychologists look at children with anti-social behaviors and post-traumatic stress, they often find insecure attachment in the parent-child relationship.

Although childhood attachment is related to some adult patterns, it does not control or determine those patterns. Whatever our early experiences may have been, as we learn more about the commitment process and remove some of its mystery, we can begin to make self-aware choices that get us closer to our most important goals.

To commit to other people is an important experience for survival, but our commitment instinct goes beyond interpersonal relations. It's also natural to become committed to a course of

---

* Over the years these concepts of attachment have gone by various names. My discussion here covers only the basics of a long and deep body of literature.

action. Take, for example, the *commitment effect*, also known as the *sunk cost fallacy*. This is the name for our tendency to stay with something not because it is the best choice, but because we have already invested time or resources into it. Among other outcomes, this effect explains why governments and individuals can end up "throwing good money after bad." Consider the guy at the county fair who's trying to win a stuffed bear at the carnival games. He may think he can shoot a few baskets or toss a few plastic rings and spend around six dollars to earn his prize. But once he's spent the six dollars and still hasn't won, does he make the rational choice to walk away? Often he continues to play, thinking that it's better to risk one more dollar to try and make up what he's already lost, becoming more deeply committed with each losing round. After a half hour he finally has the stuffed bear—at a cost of thirty-eight dollars. Some scholars argue that the commitment effect is a uniquely human and primate challenge, while others have provided evidence that even pigeons are susceptible to a form of the sunk cost fallacy. Either way, being attached to a course of action and determined to continue with it, for good or for bad, comes fairly naturally to us.

Commitment doesn't require superhuman strength. As you become more mindful of how attachment and commitment work in both yourself and others, you can make choices that better reflect your relationship, career, and lifestyle goals. By changing the variables in the commitment equation, you can turn the dial up or down on your level of commitment, depending on what you're trying to accomplish. This process begins with debunking the central myths about commitment we've been led to believe.

The 7 Commitment Myths

There are seven myths that limit our ability to see what commitment is, how it works, and the impact it has on our lives. The ability to help yourself and others consciously commit requires busting these myths.

Myth #1: Commitment—you either have it or you don't.

The way we talk about commitment often leads us to think in black-and-white terms. How often do we say, "You're either committed or you're not"? But commitment, as it turns out, is not like being pregnant; you can be a little committed.

Commitment is more like being hungry. You can be peckish or you can be famished, or you can be somewhere in between. Like most aspects of human experience, commitment is best understood as a matter of degrees. Think dimmer switch rather than on-off switch.

When conducting research on commitment, scholars typically ask people to indicate their commitment level on a scale. A survey might ask men and women in relationships to rate the degree to which they agree with the following statements, from *not at all* to *extremely*:

"I cannot imagine ending my relationship with X."

"I view my relationship with X as permanent."

"Even when X is hard to deal with, I remain committed."

Relationship researchers Leslie Baxter and Connie Bullis pointed out that movement toward higher and lower levels of commitment doesn't happen over time in a smooth upward trajectory. Instead, in the course of a developing relationship there are key turning points—those moments or experiences that significantly increase or decrease a couple's level of commitment and satisfaction. A typical pattern might be: first date (20 percent committed), first kiss (jump to 40 percent committed), meeting each other's parents (55 percent committed), ex-boyfriend shows up (dip to 45 percent committed), decision to be exclusive (up to 65 percent committed), deciding to take a break (drop to 35 percent committed), planning the wedding (way up to 95 percent committed), and so on.

There is a problem with thinking commitment is all-or-nothing, that you either "have it or you don't." There are going to be days when your commitment wavers. Days you question your professional goals or intimate relationship. Days you wonder why you made the choices you made. If your mind-set is that commitment is all-or-nothing, a temporary and natural downturn in commitment can cause you to panic. I have a friend, for example, who, when her commitment to her education wanes, starts to beat herself up: "What is wrong with me? Why can't I do this? I guess I'm just not cut out for this." And it's this reaction—and not the temporary reduction in commitment—that can cause the most trouble. You may make drastic and devastating decisions in the midst of panic that don't reflect what you really want. It's important to know that a low level of commitment doesn't automatically doom a goal, relationship, or project unless you take a drastic action that can't be taken back.

Commitment is not all-or-nothing. Varying levels of commitment in us and in others is natural and should not be alarming. It might be helpful, however, to have a strategy to successfully manage these occurrences so they don't impact you negatively. Remembering the bigger picture—a picture you'll gain from this book—will help.

Myth #2: Commitment—the moment when it all begins.

We often assume commitment occurs at the beginning of something, such as a goal. Inspirational quotations about commitment may lead us to think this way. For example, business author Les Brown wrote, "You need to make a commitment, and once you make it, then life will give you some answers." It's a thoughtful and encouraging sentiment, but it sounds as if commitment is a starting point, a beginning, rather than an outcome of critical factors.

Let's take a closer look at this belief, with your personal experience as a guide. Why do you commit to something? Why do you feel attached to a professional goal or social activity and intend to continue? Do you make that decision right at the beginning, before you have information or experience? Or does commitment develop and strengthen as you identify with the goal and invest in it? While it may be possible to become committed with one initial decision, for most people, most of the time, commitment is a process. And as you'll learn, sometimes that process is unconscious.

Recall that commitment is not the same as a promise. You can really mean it when you promise yourself you will go jogging three days a week, but that still won't be enough to get you out the door when it's cold and drizzly one week later. For that, you'll need commitment. Commitment can actually occur without an initial promise or resolution, like when you've been buying Apple computers so long you can't imagine using any other brand. It's best to think of a promise as the *potential beginning* of a commitment—it may lead naturally to commitment, and it may not. Distinguished Yale psychologist Robert Sternberg describes the experience of a couple in their sixties. On their second honeymoon they thought of their wedding day and realized that back then they'd had no idea how committed they could be. Sure, they'd stated their vows, but now those vows had a different meaning, so much deeper than when they'd said them initially. At the time they had just been words and hopes. It took many years to see the concrete result of living those words.

Let's look at a few examples to clarify the difference between a promise or an agreement, and a commitment. Remember, a promise is the potential start of something, while commitment is an attachment to a goal that shows up in action. If you understand this difference, you'll be ahead of most.

A Promise:

- Saying "I do" on your wedding day.
- Saying, "Yes, I'll join the baseball team, count me in."
- Accepting a new job.
- Joining a gym.

A Commitment:

- Always attending your kid's sporting events, even when it's inconvenient.
- Regularly buying organic produce from your local farm, even though it's more expensive.
- Staying at the same company for eighteen years and telling everyone you are proud to work there.
- Ignoring the flirtations of a sexy new coworker because you have a special someone at home.

It's helpful to see the difference between the initial words and the expression of commitment over time. Many people think that if they simply decide to commit, then like magic they will be committed and get the associated benefits. But forty years of psychological data and two centuries of economic research show that commitment is actually the outcome of everyday mental decisions and actions.

Commitment isn't what we start with; it's the result when critical factors line up.

Myth #3: Commitment—you only have to do it once.

Well-known leadership blogger Dan Rockwell once tweeted, "Commitment is a decision you don't have to make again." This idea struck a chord with his followers, who retweeted it many times. His proposal was a freeing idea, no doubt. In a society filled with too many options, distractions, and demands, it's nice to think that you can make an important decision and then never have to work at it or revisit it again. But here's the question: Is this true?

Kent was highly committed as a professor at his university.* He felt the daily pride of being a member of the college, and he garnered accolades for his research. He had no intention of leaving the university. One day, something unexpected happened, when his department hired a new faculty member. She was still nine months from finishing her PhD. Kent had earned a PhD seven years prior and had worked at the university ever since. The problem? The (not even) freshly minted PhD was hired at a significantly higher salary than Kent was making.

When Kent realized the inequity of the situation, he expressed

---

* When I use a first name only, it is a pseudonym. I am either protecting someone's privacy or referring to a composition of several people. When I use a first and last name, I am referring to a specific person.

his concern to the administration. When he was told, "We have to pay that salary to get her, and there's no money to increase current salaries," his satisfaction with his position plummeted. He started thinking about other problems and inequities that came with his post—things he had been ignoring because he was committed. Kent decided to look for a job elsewhere.

Is a commitment a decision you don't have to make again? Or, as things change, must you reevaluate and either recommit or work for change?

Thankfully there are many days you don't need to think about commitment. You continue showing up for intramural basketball even though your team always loses. You stay in your hometown even though you have complaints about the rain. And you move forward on a challenging project even though it takes you to the brink of insanity. If you contemplated every commitment every day, it would be overwhelming.

But there are times, potentially heartbreaking times, when even your most deeply held commitments come into question. It's up to you not to *will* yourself to be committed, but to look at the factors that affect your level of commitment and decide which of those factors can be adjusted and which can't. It's up to you to decide whether you're willing to work to stay committed, or whether you'd rather take the necessary steps to de-commit and choose something new. Knowing the variables that make up commitment will help you process new information and make practical choices that increase the likelihood that you can stay committed, or when necessary, walk away. Commitment is not only a decision. It's a process.

Myth #4: Commitment—the more the better.

We have a cultural philosophy that says people who are highly committed are virtuous, and people with low levels of commitment are flawed. I'd like to question that ethos, and suggest that a high level of commitment is positive or negative depending on the situation. Take the example of commitment to work. Most of us would agree that the more committed you are to your job—the more you are willing to work hard despite difficulties—the better off you will be, financially and emotionally. But what about a situation like Kendra's?

Kendra was a highly committed real estate agent for twelve years. She worked in a city that was devastated by the mortgage crisis and subsequent economic downturn. Through no direct fault of her own, Kendra's financial world was negatively impacted. Her savings was exhausted and she had to move into an apartment above her dad's garage. During some months she made a little income, but other months, after accounting for her costs, she lost money. Nonetheless, she wouldn't change course. The job was all she'd known, and it used to be very financially rewarding. Related opportunities came and went, but Kendra was convinced she didn't have the skills or aptitude for anything else. Does she just need to be more committed? To try harder and spend more of her time, energy, and resources to achieve excellence in her field? After all, the more commitment the better. Unless it isn't.

Many of us, having already tried everything—twice—have decided that the next step is to try it all again, harder. Many of us have stuck it out in some area and watched as the meaning in our lives drifted away, while we ignored other good choices. Many of us have remained committed simply because we've decided that's what a virtuous person would do, but maybe being virtuous isn't a good enough reason. Maybe what's more important is whether our interaction with a particular person or activity generates value and meaning. And if it doesn't, maybe it's okay to let go and move on.

While I was writing this book, people sometimes commented, "You're an expert on commitment, huh? You must be really committed all the time." My answer was no. Being super committed to every opportunity or person is not the point. The idea is to select specific areas of our lives that deserve greater commitment, and to learn which areas to let go of. It's as important to know how to get out of a commitment as it is to get into one. Commitment has two faces. It can free us to focus on what we want and value, but it can also constrain us and lead us to do things that are no longer in our best interest.

In Kendra's case, her unquestioning commitment was leading her to lose money by the day and overlook other choices. Perhaps she would have benefited from loosening her grip on her commitment just enough to see what she might gain if she investigated other approaches and alternatives.

Instead of a singular "more is better" attitude, we can think about how to increase or decrease commitment in the key areas of daily life with conscious intent.

Myth #5: Commitment—there's one thing to create it.

Psychologists have noticed that we tend to oversimplify the cause-and-effect process. Why am I in a bad mood? One reason: I didn't get enough sleep last night. Why didn't the candidate take the job? One reason: Someone else offered more money. Why does the neighbor complain about our yard? One reason: She's a meddling

Nellie who doesn't have enough to do. If you listen to people's attributions for why something happened, or failed to happen, the explanation is typically one-dimensional.

When it comes to understanding most aspects of social and professional life, accurate explanations are not so simple. Why am I in a bad mood? Because you snapped at me, I didn't get enough sleep, I'm behind on a project, I'm forgetting to do something but I can't think of what it is so it's nagging at me, and I had a little too much sugar on my last coffee break.

Our belief that there is one reason why people commit or fail to commit leads us to search for a single answer and stop when we find it. For example, Elizabeth Edwards left her husband, Senator John Edwards, after he admitted to having an affair. It would be tempting to say the affair was the "one reason" her commitment to the marriage dissolved, and perhaps it was. But it's interesting that other wives remain committed after learning such devastating news. If we truly want to understand these relationships—and our own—we would benefit from a more holistic view of commitment, one that accounts for a variety of factors, within which an affair or other deeply troubling incident is a part.

That our level of commitment is based on a variety of factors, and not just one, is good news. It means there are multiple paths to encouraging commitment in others and in ourselves.

Myth #6: Commitment—it brings immediate results.

It's easy to think that if you are committed, you should see results right away. If you make changes that support a new job, a new relationship, or a new way of life, you want positive outcomes to happen quickly. But while some efforts will show immediate impact, others will show it more gradually. Unfortunately, sometimes we give up before the change has had a chance to take effect, and that's why it's important to have long-term commitment.

John was the head of a team that designed everyday products using recycled materials, and he had a reputation for being cantankerous. When he missed meetings, the team actually made more progress. When he was present, he provoked arguments that included yelling and name-calling. When he attacked, it was personal and biting. On a number of occasions the more sensitive members of the group needed to take a break to compose themselves before returning to the meeting. His behavior was damaging to the group members, and some of them quit the team. Those who remained stopped sharing their best ideas for fear of being ridiculed.

Then John had a health scare, which led him to reflect on how he wanted to spend his time and energy. As a result, he slowly began to change. He became committed to modifying his management style. He stopped insulting people with personal comments. He no longer raised his voice. He started contributing to group dialogue without taking over. He began offering ideas without being aggressive. It took his team months to notice, and even longer for it to positively impact their attitude toward the effort. While many members gained a new respect for John, some couldn't believe he had changed. They figured it must be a new level of manipulation. Like the flash in our eyes that remains after a light has been turned off, we may still see, in our mind's eye, the image of the old behavior. It can take a while for perceptions to shift.

When you work to become either more or less committed, or to encourage commitment in others, the payoff is not normally instantaneous. Be patient during the process, and keep making decisions that support where you want to be. With commitment, results build with time.

Myth #7: Commitment—it's about others.

The last myth refers to where we focus our attention when we think about commitment. Often our attention is on other people rather than on ourselves, and this tendency can limit us in a few important ways.

First, it's easy to judge others who don't seem "committed enough," and we tend to be harder on them than we are on ourselves. The general tendency to focus more on the mistakes of others is so common that psychologists have given it a name: the *actor-observer bias*. A foundational concept in psychology, the actor-observer bias refers to our pattern of attributing other people's behavior to something internal, like their personality, while attributing our own behavior to something external, like the situation. This bias often occurs even when accounting for the same behavior. For example, you might find yourself thinking that your old college friend got divorced because he's no good at committing—an internal, personality reason. But when someone asks why you divorced you say, "Because of my wife's drinking"— a situational reason. It's easy to think that when a coworker shows up late to work it's because she doesn't value the organization—an internal reason. But if someone asks why you are sometimes late, you know the reason is that your kids won't get their behinds out of bed—a situational reason.

The best explanation for this unfortunate bias is that when we observe others, we focus squarely on their behavior and not on their environment. We can't see all of the forces that impact them.

On the other hand, when we observe our own behavior we focus on the environment, highly aware of what's impacting us. The result is that we may be overly harsh on others and quick to blame their character for perceived commitment failures.

Instead of judging others, it may be helpful to discover the factors that contributed to a commitment outcome. If you decide the reason the people on your team appear only 60 percent committed is because they are lazy, then you miss the opportunity to change the environment in a way that might encourage greater involvement. The truth is there are internal and external impacts on the commitment level of both you and others.

Another time we focus our attention on others is when we consider whether to make a commitment. We often have the mind-set that the reason to commit is to make others happy. This belief is understandable. It goes back to the strong connection we perceive between commitment and virtue. But let's consider whether there is something deeper about the meaning of commitment than pleasing others.

Let's look at forgiveness for a moment, because commitment and forgiveness have this myth in common. Think about who gains the most if you forgive. (And by "forgive" I don't mean you condone the person's behavior or reconcile with him—that's a different decision. We're talking about letting go of the hurtful impact that someone's behavior had on you.) It has taken time and effort for psychologists, counselors, and clergy to convince people that forgiveness actually benefits the forgiver. The other party may not even know of your forgiveness, but you are set free from the burden of hurt or resentment.

The same is true for commitment. Yes, others will benefit: team members, customers, partners, and children. But the person who will benefit most when you make conscious choices around commitment is you. There's an old saying, "Whatever you do is worth doing well." Let's add, "If you are doing something you value, it's worth finding a way to fully commit to it." It's one of the most profound ways you can enrich your own life. Commitment isn't about others; it's about you.

In this chapter we looked at the myths about commitment we've been geared to accept. These are common mind-sets like "commitment—you either have it or you don't," when in reality commitment levels vary and there's no need to panic when it wanes. Remember that commitment is a process, and you can set yourself up for greater commitment if you choose. We addressed the myth that commitment is the moment when it all begins, and saw that it's the outcome when key variables align. A promise may be the beginning, but commitment is the outcome if the right variables are present. Further, commitment isn't something you do once and forget. Instead, some of your commitments will need to be revisited. Reevaluating a commitment can be difficult, but it's easier when you know the important elements to consider. We addressed the myth that with commitment more is always better, and realized that the benefit of being highly committed is situational. Sometimes the best thing you can do is disengage and choose a new course. We dispelled the myth that only one thing creates commitment. Commitment is multidimensional. It may appear that one thing caused someone's commitment to increase or decrease, but there are always several forces that interact together to create our level of commitment. We confronted the myth that commitment brings immediate results. Deciding you are committed doesn't change things overnight. It's your commitment over time that yields results. Finally, we questioned the mind-set that commitment is about others. The real benefit of determining what deserves your commitment is a life of greater purpose and meaning.

Moving Forward

Commitment is a powerful human force that makes goal achievement possible. It isn't something you just will into existence, and it isn't something you decide on today and then forget about tomorrow. Your level of commitment varies based on some very specific elements. This journey is about bringing those elements into awareness. When you know what naturally leads to higher or lower levels of commitment, you can take steps to mindfully increase it, or learn when and how to walk away. Now that the commitment myths have been uncovered, in the next chapter we'll discuss what I call the Commitment Equation, where it came from, and how it works.

▪ CHAPTER 2 ▪

The Commitment Equation

WHY does the wife of one politician leave him after a scandalous affair, while the wife of another stands by his side for years? Why do some leaders successfully gain commitment from volunteers, while others fail to gain real commitment from their paid workforce? And why do all of us feel incredibly committed to something today, like getting back in shape, but find our resolve has weakened by tomorrow?

For years, social scientists have studied the elements, or variables, that predict commitment. Their work has shown that four variables interact to influence a person's level of commitment to just about anything: a career, sports, relationships, and more. While these elements have been called different names over the years, I refer to them as *treasures*, *troubles*, *contributions*, and *choices*. Together, I call them the Commitment Equation:

(Treasures − Troubles) + Contributions − Choices = Level of Commitment

Treasures and *troubles* interact to create your level of satisfaction, a key part of commitment. Treasures are the aspects of an activity you find rewarding and fulfilling, while troubles are the parts you find challenging or costly. Satisfaction with your career, for example, is a product of how much you treasure the aspects of your work, minus the troubles that come with it. As a university professor, an important part of my job is teaching, and I love designing high-impact activities and lessons, participating in invigorating classroom discussions, and experiencing the lasting friendships that come as a result. On the downside, I'm troubled when students spend more time worrying about their grades than they do studying the material and working on the assignments. I'm also not a fan of the mental fatigue that results from extensive grading. It's the balance between these two elements—the treasures and the troubles—that determines our level of satisfaction. Fortunately for me as an instructor, my treasures far outweigh my troubles, and satisfaction with this part of my career is high.

However, satisfaction is only part of what leads us to be committed. If commitment were about satisfaction alone, we'd stay with anything that makes us happy and walk away from everything that doesn't. Of course, we know this isn't how commitment works. Research shows that satisfaction is the most powerful predictor of commitment, but there are two additional elements that impact whether you stick with something or decide to move on.

The third variable in the equation is *contributions*. Contributions are the tangible and intangible resources you've invested in an activity or relationship that can't be fully retrieved if you walk away. They may consist of sharing your time, money, energy, effort, creativity, care, and concern. In my case, as an educator, I've contributed a lot of time and money to my training and professional development. I've also invested a large part of my identity in being an instructor, and it requires ongoing effort to remain current in my field and effective in the classroom. High levels of contribution are powerful where long-term commitment is concerned. Having made an investment, you're more likely to stay with a course of action even when satisfaction is low. Often that's a great thing, but, as we'll see, contributions can also keep you tied to an unhealthy commitment in which you give increasingly more to an activity or relationship that's no longer right for you, or downright harmful.

Choices, the fourth element of commitment, refers to the degree to which you believe you have other good options. If you see a lot of great alternatives to your current career, for example, your commitment will likely be reduced. But if you think you are unlikely to find anything better, you're more likely to stay with what you have. My options, besides teaching, include focusing exclusively on research and writing or moving to university administration. I remain committed to teaching because I don't find these other choices more attractive. Like contributions, choices can work for you or against you depending on whether you're interested in sticking with a commitment or letting it go. The belief that you have other good options is important when you want to reduce your commitment to something that's no longer working for you. But focusing too much on the options works against you when you want to keep a commitment strong. It's helpful to put the power of choice into the right context so you can consciously decide when to focus on what you already have and when to seek other options.

In short, you are most committed when your satisfaction is

high (i.e., treasures significantly exceed troubles), your contributions have been significant, and your choices seem limited.

(Treasures − Troubles) + Contributions − Choices = Level of Commitment

I didn't come up with this formula. Many great minds have contributed to understanding what drives commitment, from fields as diverse as economics and sociology. In this chapter, we'll take a historical tour and discover how researchers came to the understanding that these four variables *predict* commitment. The perspective provided here will benefit you in Chapters 3 through 6, where we will discuss the elements in detail and learn how to take your commitments to the next level in order to achieve your most important goals.

The origin of the first part of the equation, treasures minus troubles, comes from the field of economics. Although early economists were primarily concerned with market decisions—how and why individuals interact with each other when buying or selling goods and services—researchers from the social sciences realized these economic principles applied to other areas of human behavior, like commitment to personal and professional goals.

What's the Net Benefit?

The first part of commitment theory is rooted in economics and the principle of cost-benefit analysis. Let's say you want do something tens of thousands of Americans are doing today to ease their financial burden: rent out a room in your basement or above the garage. Initially, you're not thinking about renting in the context of commitment. You're thinking about the extra cash you need to pay for Junior's school clothes and some badly needed vacation time. You're also pondering what you'll have to give up, namely room for the in-laws when they visit each November. And then there's the price of the rent. You must determine a monthly rate that's high enough to be worth giving up your precious space, but low enough that someone will be willing to pay.

At first this process appears to be about simply setting a price, but it's also about generating commitment from both you and your potential renter. You wouldn't go to all the trouble of moving or storing the existing furniture and placing the rental advertisement only to change your mind before renting the unit. Nor would you cherish the idea of securing a renter who bails after three weeks, leaving only his collection of crushed Pabst beer cans and extensive Cheetos art. It's in the best interest of you and your renter to have a satisfying, long-term commitment, and this begins with a cost-benefit analysis to determine a fair price.

Formal cost-benefit analysis apparently began with talented road and bridge engineer Jules Dupuit, who, along with his contemporaries in the early 1800s, needed to determine the ideal price to charge for a toll bridge. The task, as it turned out, was not so simple. At the time, the study of economics was considered "art" rather than science, and there were no mathematical formulas for determining an optimum price. Contemplating what to charge for crossing the bridge, Dupuit reasoned that the lower the toll, the more a person would use the bridge, but the more frequently a person wanted to use it, the less money he'd be willing to pay. He plotted numbers on a graph and a downward sloping curve emerged. In 1844, Dupuit published his findings and uncovered an important element of cost-benefit analysis: *demand*. Demand in the market is based on a number of things, including what Dupuit called "the curve of diminishing marginal utility," or what is known more generally as the law of diminishing returns. When renting your extra room, for example, you must realize that the longer a potential renter is planning to stay, the less he'll be willing to pay per night. Most rental companies understand this. Go online to sites like Vacation Rentals by Owner and you'll see a discount offered for extended stays. When people commit for longer periods, they expect their costs to be reduced.

It Depends on Your Options

Even more important to commitment theory was the principle that evolved from demand: *supply*. The supply curve was added to Dupuit's demand curve in 1890 when English neoclassical economist Alfred Marshall published his book *Principles of Economics*. Marshall's supply curve reflected the idea that the more abundant a good or service, the less people will value it. Conversely, the less abundant a good or service, the more people will value it. If you're renting space and you live in Manhattan, not only is demand high; supply is limited. So economic theory predicts you're going to get a pile for your 250-square-foot room. In a small town where demand is considerably less and extra rooms are abundant, you might be lucky to rent your space for enough to cover the cable bill.

In general, we place a lower value on something when we have other good options, and we value something more when it's in short supply. Thus we may be less satisfied and committed (even to something great) when we see abundant choices. This principle affects many areas of our lives—economic decisions, certainly, but even selecting and sticking with a romantic partner. For example, the number of males and females born in the United States is essentially the same, with males slightly outnumbering females (one baby girl for every 1.05 baby boys). All things being equal, heterosexual men and women have a similar number of partners from which to choose and make a commitment. But the ratio changes when we get older. By age sixty-five, there are three men for every four women. On a three-thousand-passenger cruise hosting energetic and single retirees, you could expect an additional 430 women relative to men. These lucky fellows could be a little more selective about their shuffleboard partners given their favorable odds. The women, on the other hand, would have to bring their "A" game if they wanted to end up on a competitive team.

The influence of costs, benefits, and options isn't only applicable to market decisions. It's also applicable to personal decisions. In the 1950s, American sociologist George Homans would make this bold assertion, and the resulting insights would have game-changing implications for understanding human interaction and commitment.

It's About People

Often, in casual conversation, the language we use to describe our interactions with others indicates a kind of exchange, not between us and the market but between us and another person. How often have you heard someone say, "I took a lot of great ideas from our conversation," or "Talking with her took a lot out of me"? Homans noticed this tendency and theorized that people exchange not only material things but also nonmaterial things, like approval, support, and respect.

Let's say Ted, a lawyer, is telling jokes to Julie, a woman he's just met. She laughs at his jokes, and it encourages him to tell more. He's enjoying the exchange but also notices Julie occasionally looking over his shoulder, and he wonders if she's truly interested in talking with him. So he evaluates the situation, consciously or unconsciously, and starts to think about working the room, looking for another interaction that is more rewarding. Julie, on the other hand, is thinking Ted's jokes are funny, especially the ones about lawyers, but she desires stimulating conversation and she's not getting it from him. She considers moving on and looks over Ted's shoulder, assessing other options. But for now, she remains in an exchange with Ted because it's better than standing there alone.

Like the neoclassical economists, Homans suggested that people are rational and want to continue interaction when there is a "profitable" exchange. In satisfying relationships parties create beneficial exchanges in which the more you give, the more you receive: Neighbors exchange favors, politicians exchange concessions, and colleagues exchange assistance. Even in cultures in which the exchange of gifts appears voluntary, the practice may reflect significant obligation. Remember the last time a friend did something thoughtful for you and you felt the need to return the favor in a timely fashion? Recently, a colleague gave me her spot in a writing conference. I knew I couldn't let that go without a thank-you, so I bought her a spendy bottle of wine and hoped that was enough. That's how societies and people in relationships behave. There's an expectation of reciprocity.

One of the first to examine the hypothesis that interactions continue when there's a positive exchange for both parties was sociologist Peter Blau. Inspired by Homans, in 1964 Blau offered a simple but significant equation for human interaction: (Rewards − Costs for A) = (Rewards − Costs for B).

These ideas became generally known as *social exchange*. Social exchange is relatively subtle, but once you learn about it, Blau said, you'll begin to see it everywhere. Consider Twitter, for example, the social networking site. Twitter is an Internet-based medium in which "following back" and "retweeting" are valued commodities. If you are friends with Ted the lawyer and you regularly retweet his jokes and congratulate him on his various successes, you might expect him to respond with a thank-you and maybe a compliment in return. If Ted fails to respond in kind, you may wonder whether you are indeed friends and, eventually, you may decide to give up on the interaction altogether. In the spirit of social exchange, a number of applications have been developed to help you identify people who have stopped following you, so you can immediately stop following them.

Social exchange is different from economic exchange because it consists not only of concrete rewards like money but also of intrinsic rewards like approval, support, friendship, and gratitude. These intrinsic rewards, Blau wrote, can mean as much as or more than material rewards. But since they haven't been given an economic value, we must make an internal determination about whether the exchange is better or worse than we could get somewhere else. Each of us has only so much time, energy, and resources to share, so we have to make choices about where to commit ourselves in work, love, and life.

We know from our discussion thus far that our level of satisfaction, and ultimately our level of commitment, depends in large part on how beneficial the exchange is, relative to our other options. But there is one more element of commitment to be revealed.

The Power of a Side Bet

You and your renter agree that the exchange is beneficial, and you believe each is committed to the agreed-upon terms. The rental price is fair and the room suits your tenant's needs. She's considered her other options and believes your space is the best choice available. You've both considered not only the economic exchange but also the social exchange, acknowledging that respect and kindness matter as much as an exchange of services. So since it's a satisfying exchange all around, why would you and your tenant need to sign a lease agreement? A rational analysis of costs and benefits should be enough to generate commitment, should it not? Intuitively, you already know the answer. You and your tenant need to sign the lease because your commitment to the deal isn't only based on satisfaction; it's also based on having something to lose if you walk away. The lease agreement will state the repercussions of leaving, and when you sign on the dotted line it's like making a bet you'll stay committed.

In 1960, sociologist Howard Becker made the first attempt among modern social scientists to identify why people consciously or unconsciously commit to a course of action beyond a cost-benefit analysis. The resulting insight is that we are more committed when we involve an outside interest, something Becker referred to as a *side bet*. Let's say you want to lose twenty pounds and you join a fitness club. Over a beer that night, your friend says to you,

"I don't think you can lose twenty pounds. You drink too much beer." You immediately bet him a hundred dollars that you will lose the weight, and within three months. You've just done something to increase your commitment: You brought in the side bet of a hundred dollars. A bet like this encourages you to stay committed because you've contributed something you don't want to lose.

Side bets aren't always explicit, nor do they necessarily involve money. A side bet occurs anytime you do something that increases the consequences, or losses, of not staying with it. A common side bet is simply telling people, "I'm committed." When you announce your intention in this way, the side bet is your reputation, trustworthiness, or self-image. Consider marriage. Does publicly announcing your intention to remain married until death increase the likelihood that you will do so? Absolutely. Commitment isn't only about treasuring what you have; it's also about avoiding perceived negative outcomes of deserting the commitment. This latter component may be more motivating than we realize. "Decisions not supported by side bets will lack staying power," Becker wrote. We strongly encourage our own commitment—for good or bad—when we contribute material or psychological side bets.

A similar concept was proposed by social psychologist Jeffrey Rubin in the 1970s. He called it *entrapment*. He said people stay with a course of action during a conflict and become increasingly committed to their line of reasoning once they have invested something. For good or bad, they stay the course and attempt to make good on the time, energy, or money they've already contributed. Sociologist Louis Kriesberg explained it like this: "We all experience entrapment when we are put on hold when telephoning or when we wait for a bus; the longer we wait the more we want to walk away but the more reluctant we are to do so, having already invested so much time."

Becker reasoned that these investments are why we sometimes find ourselves backing into a commitment without conscious intent. We make a series of small decisions that singularly seem to mean very little, but that taken together serve to continue a course of action. Consider a young man who shares personal stories with a casual date—no big deal. He helps her adopt a dog—you know, just being nice. Later, he tells a few friends about the young woman, and they start asking questions. The couple begins dating on a regular basis; they're now an item. A few months later, they move in together to split the bills, and he's committed without ever having intended it. Committed by default, Becker would say; rather than by design, I might add.

So here's what we know so far. We understand from economic principles that market decisions are the result of analyzing the costs and benefits, or the treasures and troubles, of our perceived choices. We learn from sociology that these principles apply not only to economic decisions, but to personal decisions as well. We also learn from sociologists that commitment isn't just about making a rational cost-benefit decision. We are more likely to stay with a course of action because we've contributed something, maybe a side bet we don't want to lose. We know these decisions can be made consciously, but we also know they can be made unconsciously through a series of small contributions that accumulate over time.

We've learned a lot, but do these economic and sociological findings actually *predict* our level of commitment? To test whether these variables have a real effect on commitment, we move to the social psychologists.

A Relationship Formula

The economic conceptualization of costs, benefits, options, and exchange would provide insights for relationship researchers. While historically social scientists hadn't studied experiences like love and attraction, in the 1970s a group of psychologists became determined to apply the same mathematical rigor of the other sciences to the study of human bonding. In 1978 two of the pioneers in this field, Harold Kelley and John Thibaut, formalized social exchange as a way of understanding how people develop and maintain relationships. Like the sociologists, Thibaut and Kelley theorized that your level of satisfaction in a relationship is based on how much the rewards of the relationship exceed the costs. But like the economists, they included the idea of supply. They suggested that whether you believe you have good alternatives also matters. They called this your "comparison level to alternatives." What Thibaut and Kelley suggested is that your past personal experience, your observation of other relationships, and your imagination about what it would be like to be with someone else all affect how satisfied you are in your current relationship. The perceived quality of your choices can lead you to be unsatisfied in a perfectly healthy relationship or, conversely, thrilled in a so-so relationship. Their equation is: Satisfaction = (Rewards − Costs) − Alternatives.

Even in satisfying relationships there are trade-offs. There are things we have to do that we might not enjoy so our partner will feel rewarded. In relationships that persist, however, participants typically have a higher degree of *correspondence*. This means what is rewarding to you is also rewarding to your partner, and what's costly to you is also costly to your partner. A couple has correspondence when he likes to travel for business and she's happy to have some time to herself. A boss and employee have correspondence when the employee likes a lot of feedback and the boss likes to give it. When people talk about "compatibility," they are often referring to correspondence.

Thibaut and Kelley became well known in their field for conceptualizing social exchange as a way of understanding why people are drawn to personal relationships. They hinted at commitment when they said people are more likely to stay in a relationship when the reward-cost value of the relationship is superior to that of alternative relationships. But it took their star graduate student, Caryl Rusbult,[*] to address commitment explicitly.

Adding It Up

Utilizing the principles of social exchange, along with Becker's side bet concept and Rubin's notion of entrapment, in 1980 Rusbult published a framework called the Investment Model, which *statistically predicted commitment levels by measuring specific variables*. The first variable she included is a person's level of *satisfaction* with the relationship. Recall that satisfaction comes from the degree to which rewards outweigh costs, or treasures outweigh troubles. The second variable of the model is the degree to which a person has attractive *alternatives* to her current relationship. A person's level of commitment decreases when she perceives good alternative choices, and it increases when she perceives fewer alternatives. The third variable included in the model is called *investments*. Rusbult had the insight to apply Becker and Rubin's ideas about staying with a course of

---

* "Caryl" is pronounced like "Carol."

action to staying with a relationship. A person is more committed when he contributes tangible things like time and money, and intangible things like sharing personal information. The more he contributes to the relationship, the more likely he is to want to stay and make good on the investment. Alternatively, if he's contributed very little to a relationship, it's easier to walk away.

Each of these variables individually influences commitment, but when combined, they become a powerful tool that statistically predicts commitment levels. Rusbult's work is often summarized in research articles with visual models similar to this:

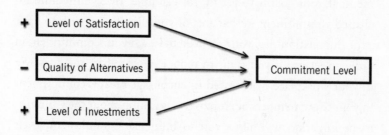

By 2003, more than fifty studies had used Rusbult's model to predict levels of commitment in a variety of contexts, from relationships to organizations to sports. A meta-analysis of these studies showed that, statistically, these variables accounted for almost two-thirds of a person's decision to commit. In the social sciences, that's a huge number. It means once we learn about these variables, why we commit will be less of a mystery and more in our control. The meta-analysis also showed that the elements are interdependent. For example, if you've contributed a lot to your career, you'll want to see that career as satisfying, and thus you'll be less attracted to other choices. So changing how you think or act in even one area can have large implications for your overall level of commitment.

Using the Commitment Equation

The intention of the social science research has been to explain the why of human behavior, and we'll be investigating that as well. We'll also consider how we can use the Commitment Equation to meet personal and professional goals. Just as concrete and rebar form the essential foundation of a house, where you choose to commit yourself provides the foundation and structure of your life. If you're like a lot of people, you have plenty of goals, and to achieve these goals you must build a strong foundation of commitment. If your goal is to get fit, for example, that will require increased commitment in that area of your life. If you wish to leave a hurtful relationship, you will need to lessen your commitment in order to let go. If you want to reduce absenteeism and turnover in your workplace, you'll need to encourage greater commitment in your team members or employees. Learning about the Commitment Equation will allow you to influence commitment levels where it matters most.

The previous examples reflect three common commitment goals we experience throughout our lives. I refer to these goals as "all in," "moving on," and "assisting others." An "all in" commitment goal occurs when you want a higher level of commitment from yourself in some area of your life. Maybe you realize you're not as devoted to your career as you would like, and as a result you aren't doing your best work. You want to gain the benefits that will come from a higher level of commitment within yourself. A "moving on" commitment goal reflects your desire to decrease your attachment to something. Perhaps you are in a social circle that just isn't right, but for a variety of reasons you have a hard time letting go of it. You want to know what you can change so it's easier to walk away. The third commitment goal is "assisting others" to increase their level of commitment. Let's say you are a volunteer coordinator and you want to develop commitment among the new recruits so you can count on their continued support. Knowledge of the Commitment Equation can help you do just that. A less common commitment goal is to assist others in reducing or eliminating their commitment to something unhealthy or that is causing them harm. An example is a counselor who wants to help a client reduce her attachment to an unhealthy relationship. As we discuss the equation you may also realize there are times you are inadvertently encouraging lower levels of commitment in the people around you, and that's good to know. In that case, knowledge of the commitment predictors will give you some ideas for changing your behavior if decreased commitment in others is not your intent.

Moving Forward

In this chapter, you learned that commitment has been investigated for many years and from several different fields of study, culminating in the insight from Caryl Rusbult that key variables statistically predict levels of commitment in a variety of circumstances—variables I call treasures, troubles, contributions, and choices. Now it's time to understand these time-tested principles and determine how we can use them to generate commitment to our valued goals.

· PART II ·

The Elements of Commitment

CHAPTER 3

Treasures: What Do You Value?

(Treasures – Troubles) + Contributions – Choices = Level of Commitment

WHEN she was young, my friend Kris King had many talents, but no occupational focus. She worked at a variety of jobs, but nothing that truly fulfilled her. Then, in her midthirties, she got some news that would lead to tremendous change in her life—change that would positively impact her career track and sense of purpose. It began with what most of us would consider a tragedy. Kris learned she had breast cancer and that she needed not only a year of chemotherapy but also a mastectomy.

Kris was determined to heal—not only her physical health, but her state of mind and how she lived her life. She began exercising and reading self-improvement books, and she radically changed her diet. Then a trusted friend recommended a personal development course and, seeking anything that would help, she signed right up. During this seminar she made some big discoveries; paramount was that deep inside she'd been holding other people accountable for her choices and emotions. Now, with the insights she'd gained from the training, Kris had the power to take ownership of her life, both personally and professionally.

She discovered her career path as what she calls a "transformational educator." Although she didn't have the credentials and didn't feel ready, she was passionate about the goal of becoming a trainer to assist others with personal and professional development. She enrolled in classes, volunteered, and committed to her own improvement. After a year and a half, she was thrilled to receive a job offer from the very company that had helped her begin to change her life. She started in marketing and soon became a trainer. After working with the company for two years, Kris was given the opportunity to become an owner. Neither she nor her new business partner had any cash, but Kris's determination led her to mortgage her home. She had become the co-owner of a respected company, doing what she loved.

But how long would she stay with it? The economy can be particularly hard on small businesses, and after a few years, she and her business partner split. Since then she has remortgaged her house several times to keep the company afloat. But today it's been more than twenty-five years and Kris and her company are still here. She has remained uncompromisingly committed, and the company continues to positively impact the lives of thousands of people every year.

How has Kris remained so deeply committed to her goal of doing this work despite the financial challenges? The answer comes down to this: Every day she treasures the rewards that come from running her company. She always remembers what the commitment has done for her personally. Thirty-three years after chemotherapy and a second mastectomy, Kris is the only person from her treatment group still living. She attributes her physical resilience to doing the work she loves. And she never stops appreciating the positive feedback from the people whose lives she has impacted. Confronted with ongoing financial risk, Kris never doubts her commitment. Instead, she focuses her energy on the work she treasures.

The Meaning of Treasures

Kris's story provides an example of the relationship between high levels of commitment and the first element of the equation: *treasures*. Kris wanted purpose and meaning in her life, and when she found a career that fit, she fully invested herself. Focusing on what you value about an activity generates the resilience and creativity you need to deal with the inevitable problems and obstacles.

In the previous chapter you saw that rewards or treasures are the aspects of an activity you find desirable or fulfilling. In a relationship, you may treasure the in-jokes, physical intimacy, and financial stability. In your career, you may treasure a steady paycheck, feelings of accomplishment, and a company-paid parking space. In an education context, you might treasure good grades, the camaraderie of students and faculty, and the sense of a bright future.

Social scientists have historically used the words *rewards* and *benefits*, as opposed to *treasures*, because the origin of these commitment elements came from the field of economics. I will use these terms at times as well, but I prefer to conceptualize our most cherished rewards—those that truly mean something to us—as treasures because it does a better job of capturing the joy or fulfillment that comes from engaging in something worthwhile.

The simple reality about treasures is "the more the better." The more we treasure something, the stronger our commitment will be to the source that provides it, even when inevitable challenges arise. But social science research also shows that treasures impact our level of commitment in more subtle and complex ways. Here's what we know:

1. Rewards are both internal (intrinsic) and external (extrinsic), but over time, intrinsic rewards have a stronger effect on commitment.
2. We treasure rewards more when they are fair in relation to what others receive.
3. We treasure both expected and unexpected rewards, but the unexpected, random rewards have a greater impact on commitment.
4. We treasure unique rewards, especially when we don't think we can get them elsewhere.
5. Treasures are subjective and personal. To understand what others treasure we must see from their perspective.

In this chapter we'll look at the impactful and often unseen factors that affect whether, and how much, you treasure a relationship, job, or activity. We'll also identify ways to increase the rewards that matter for high levels of commitment in yourself and others.

Intrinsic and Extrinsic Treasures

As a culture we like to focus on the concrete external rewards that come with a job or a relationship. Every day we hear stories of men and women who have yachts, mansions, and sex tapes as a result of their occupation or whom they married. These are examples of *extrinsic treasures*—the beneficial outcomes of an activity, job, or relationship. In the real world of work and love, extrinsic treasures more likely include getting a raise and promotion, or dating someone who's willing do the dishes or mow the lawn. While extrinsic treasures are important to developing commitment, for many people they are not enough. *Intrinsic treasures* are the elements of an activity or relationship that are inherently rewarding, rather than material gains you receive as an outcome. If you play a sport, intrinsic treasures likely include the spirit of competition, or increased energy and focus. If you write a blog, you probably gain the intrinsic treasure of expressing yourself and connecting with others. In your career, intrinsic treasures may include a sense of accomplishment or mastering your craft.

We are motivated by both intrinsic and extrinsic rewards, but when it comes to a lasting commitment, the intrinsic is particularly important. This is a trend in many areas of our lives, like work, exercise, and love.

The Power of Intrinsic Treasures at Work

If you think about the places you've held a job, it's likely you felt a deeper connection with some organizations than with others. Perhaps there was an organization where you felt quite bonded, and proudly wore your company's logo T-shirt on the weekend (we've all seen these people). In other organizations you may have felt no connection at all. You were only there for the paycheck (an extrinsic treasure) and couldn't wait to get out and work somewhere new. The degree to which you bonded or identified with your workplace is called *organizational commitment*, and the consensus among researchers is that your level of commitment to an organization is fairly static. That is, it doesn't change much from one day to the next. How *satisfied* you are with your job, however, can vary quite a bit. You can love your job one day and think it's a drag the next, all the while feeling high levels of commitment to the company. Because organizational commitment predicts both employee effort and turnover, businesses are certainly interested in having a committed workforce. Sadly, record numbers of us currently want to quit our jobs, and too many of us who stay are actively disengaged from the work. We'll be more committed when we experience our work, like Kris King does, as intrinsically rewarding.

Two professionals—Brian Joo, a professor of human resources, and Taejo Lim, a leadership development manager—found that three intrinsic treasures are associated with greater organizational commitment: *job complexity*, *task importance*, and *autonomy*. If you want to go all in at work or assist others in doing the same, consider whether these treasures are present, or if they can be created.

Job complexity refers to whether employees feel like they are being challenged, working with interesting questions, and utilizing their skills and creativity. Joo and Lim found that proactive people were more likely to consider their job complex because they actively looked for challenges that allowed them to apply their skills in new and creative ways. As an example, let's visit your local hair salon. At first glance, you might think cutting someone's hair isn't an especially complex job. But for a proactive professional hairstylist it's a different story. My hairdresser, Kim Mitchell-Clyde, experiences her job as highly complex. She says that the client's desire for something new, along with current fashions and trends, means "the stylist must make an artistic, technical, and sometimes emotional decision on a course of action, usually in five minutes or less." Then during the cut itself "there is the technical, geometric aspect of the cut and color and also the social interaction, which is often quite emotional." In part because she experiences her job as complex, Kim is intrinsically rewarded by her work. She's committed too, having been in the trade for eighteen years. As a co-owner of the salon, it's important for Kim to relay this complexity to the new stylists she brings on.

Task importance is the second intrinsic treasure associated with higher commitment, and it refers to whether employees feel they are doing meaningful work. No one wants to feel like they are only going through the motions. We want to feel like what we do matters. Of course, many of our daily tasks don't seem all that important. Both employees and employers can learn to identify the ways in which even routine tasks are significant in the larger picture. For example, being a hairdresser is much more than styling hair. This seemingly basic task represents a larger purpose. Kim recalls the history of the beauty salon as a place where women gathered to share information in the absence of formal education. Today hairdressers facilitate a safe environment where customers' hardships are listened to and supported. Kim sees the styling of hair as a mechanism to what's truly important—a woman's well-being.

Autonomy, the third intrinsic treasure associated with commitment, refers to whether employees are allowed and encouraged to approach their jobs in the way they see fit. There are limits to granting autonomy, but whenever a leader can allow employees, students, or team members to make autonomous decisions, those folks are more likely to see value in what they do—value that translates into increased commitment. Many stylists work in someone else's salon, but they often operate as independent business entities renting a workstation, rather than traditional employees. This means they have autonomy regarding the hours they work, the technical and artistic techniques they will use, and how they will apply them in their own creative way. For Kim, "as long as the boundaries of professionalism and respect are intact," each stylist is free to do her work in the way she sees fit.

According to the studies documented in Daniel Pink's *Drive*, once people are being paid fairly—when that baseline extrinsic reward is covered—they want something intrinsically rewarding. If you lead or manage and want to assist others to achieve greater commitment, it's important to understand the kinds of rewards the people in your workplace treasure. People appear to be more committed when they are provided with opportunities to do jobs that are challenging and tasks that are important, and when they have some flexibility in how they do it.

Finding a job intrinsically rewarding makes a difference at work. But how will intrinsic treasures make a difference in situations beyond work—say, exercise?

The Power of Intrinsic Treasures in Fitness and Sports

Many people will tell you the reason they exercise is for extrinsic treasures, like seeing the number on the scale go down or getting their doctor to stop bothering them about cholesterol. We tend to encourage others to commit to exercise by pointing out the extrinsic benefits they'll attain, like living longer and fitting into their favorite jeans. To what degree is a focus on extrinsic outcomes successful?

To investigate, let's go to Greece, the birthplace of the gymnasium. Gymnasiums in ancient times were primarily a training space for physical activity, but they were also considered a social hub. Here the men (it was ancient Greece, after all) engaged in intellectual and philosophical discussions, and the gymnasium meeting place was an important part of the community. Fast-forward to today's fitness centers, where individuals bob along on computerized treadmills or stair-climbers while independently plugged in to music or a television show. The most connection you'll see at some of these places is one weight lifter asking another for a "spot" so he doesn't drop two hundred pounds on his head.

Figures vary, but the average fitness facility experiences a minimum turnover of 40 percent of its customer base each year. All told, most people who begin a fitness program stop. Many medical professionals and researchers are concerned and confused about our collective lack of commitment to exercise. It seems that all the information about the importance of exercise to our personal and collective health should have made a difference by now. Plenty of people certainly begin an exercise program or sport because they've been told it's good for them. But commitment means being psychologically attached to the activity and resolved to continue.

Researchers in Greece wanted to discover what separates members who are highly committed to their health club from those who are less committed. Data was collected in three randomly selected private fitness facilities, where the majority of participants happened to be women. The number one thing that predicted commitment was *feeling involved* with the club. That's right, feeling involved—not losing body fat. Highly committed members enjoyed their instructors, the front desk people, and the opportunities for friendship. They valued formal and informal communication that kept them connected to what was going on. They felt their club provided opportunities to be involved—opportunities they didn't think they were likely to find somewhere else.

A 2012 *New York Times* article questioned the strategy of encouraging people to commit to exercise by focusing exclusively on health benefits while ignoring other important elements. Doctors and trainers are good at educating people about the positive physical outcomes of proper exercise, but according to Rod Dishman, director of the exercise psychology laboratory at the University of Georgia, that tactic may work only in the short run. Commitment can fade because "people don't feel their bones getting stronger, they don't feel lipids changing, they don't feel their blood pressure changing." All these things are extrinsic rewards—they occur as a result of the activity. They aren't something we experience and treasure internally.

While there is currently little research on commitment to exercise among adults, there is a lot of data on youth. Take all those young competitive soccer players in Spain. While extrinsic rewards like trophies and winning games are important, the intrinsic rewards like friendship and personal fulfillment contribute more to their level of commitment. In fact, a study of U.S. youth in a variety of competitive sports, including basketball and volleyball, found that extrinsic rewards had no effect on commitment at all; it was all about intrinsic rewards. Consider an example of what one college football coach does to encourage intrinsic rewards.

Chris Petersen is the head football coach at Boise State University. Coach Pete, as he is affectionately known, has at the time of this writing an 84-8 win/loss record and five bowl-game victories (including two BCS Fiesta Bowls), and is a two-time Paul "Bear" Bryant Award recipient. As one of the most successful college football coaches in the nation, Coach Petersen understands a few things about gaining commitment from his players. In a recent interview, he told me he seeks to provide all of his players with three intrinsic treasures that greatly contribute to the team's success and the development of each individual: building self-esteem, adding value to their lives, and enjoying the process.

The intrinsic treasure of increased self-esteem comes down to how the players are coached. "You'll find a lot of coaches that yell and scream and get in their face," says Petersen. "But if something went wrong, that's the coach's responsibility. Don't yell at the kid. You have to ask, 'Is the way you're talking to that kid going to make him feel good about himself? Is it going to make him feel like he's improving and he's learning and can see himself getting better?' I look for assistant coaches that can connect with the kids, set them up for success. It's not just about X's and O's; it's about making that connection."

In order to add value to their lives, the coaches take advantage of teachable moments that help team members grow as people, not just as players. On their 2010 opening game against Virginia Tech in Washington, D.C., the coaches took time out of the trip so the players could see the White House and war memorials and get personally introduced to those important pieces of our country's history. Similarly, when they went to Hawaii in 2012, the whole team went to Pearl Harbor for several hours so the players could understand what happened there. The way Petersen and his staff see it, football is a platform to help these young men reach their full potential.

The intrinsic treasure of enjoying the process means taking time out from their grinding work to be in the moment and bond as a team. During fall camp, for example, they will do something fun to break up practice days, like floating the river as a team. Or after a great series of practices, Petersen has let an ice cream truck into the stadium to treat the guys to a cone after practice. The idea is, even though the work is incredibly hard, there should always be opportunities to stop and enjoy the moment.

All great teams require immense commitment, and while extrinsic outcomes like a strong win-lose record or getting on the cover of *Sports Illustrated* are certainly rewarding, the process must offer intrinsic benefits as well. Petersen's triad—building self-esteem, adding value to their lives, and enjoying the process—goes a long way toward helping the players treasure their football experience.

If you are one of the many people who have started and then stopped an exercise program, you might consider whether you were focused on intrinsic or extrinsic rewards. Have you ever picked an exercise or sport because you thought it was the "best" from a health or beauty perspective, even though the activity wasn't fun or fulfilling? Have you then felt guilty for losing interest and letting your commitment slide? There is a way out of this annoying cycle: looking for activities that are intrinsically rewarding to you. Research has shown that intrinsic values like enjoying the activity and connecting with others are associated with higher commitment, and that applies to sustaining a workout routine as well. Going for an exercise that has intrinsic rewards may require a little experimentation. You may need to try a number of activities over a period of time. But the effort will be worth it when you find an exercise you really do enjoy and your commitment comes more easily and naturally.

The Power of Intrinsic Treasures in Relationships

When it comes to relationships, the relative value of extrinsic or intrinsic treasures appears to depend on the nature of the relationship. Some relationships are what you might call *tit-for-tat* relationships. When you ask your coworker if she will sub for you at the restaurant on Friday night and she responds, "Yeah, but you're going to have to sub for me next weekend," you can see the relationship is tit for tat. She doesn't intrinsically treasure the opportunity to help you; rather, she wants an external payoff. Similarly, in tit-for-tat relationships you may withhold extrinsic benefits when they are withheld from you. Your roommate asks why you didn't clean your mess in the kitchen and you say, "Because you left your stuff all over the living room." Again, it's tit for tat.

In relationships with greater commitment, you are less likely to explicitly exchange external rewards, and more likely to give what your partner needs because it feels intrinsically good to do so. Social scientists call this a *communal* relationship. If you mow your grandmother's yard every Saturday, it's unlikely you expect her to come to your home on Monday to return the favor. You do it because it feels good to know you made her life a little easier. In return, your grandmother might surprise you by baking an apple pie for you to take home. Grandma is similarly rewarded. She feels good that you love her apple pie, and she wants to make sure you have the energy to come back next week. Although there are extrinsic benefits involved here, the true exchange is intrinsic.

There are reasons why committed relationships tend to be more communal and less tit-for-tat. One reason is practicality—over time it becomes difficult to keep track of everybody's contributions. In communal relationships it's more helpful to trust that both people are contributing as much as they can to the other and the relationship. Another reason, which is well documented, is that in highly committed relationships we experience a kind of cognitive overlap between us and our partner. We don't make as large a distinction between self and other as we do in less significant relationships. Researchers measure this cognitive overlap by asking people in relationships to draw a Venn diagram in which one circle represents the self and the other circle represents the partner. In committed partnerships, people draw circles with a greater degree of overlap, as if the mental distinction between them and their partner is blurred. You may have noticed that when you are in a close relationship and something positive or negative happens to your partner, it almost feels like the event happened to you. In these kinds of relationships, to meet your partner's needs is intrinsically rewarding. To help him or her is also to help yourself and the relationship.

Of course, even committed relationships can revert to periods of tit for tat. When satisfaction and trust decline, one or both partners may withhold benefits, like giving affection or completing a chore, until they get something tangible first. When both people do this, the relationship ends up in a stalemate. To move through this period—and get back to intrinsic treasures and higher commitment—consider two things. First, begin by contributing something small to the relationship—an unexpected note, treat, or favor—without expecting anything in return. Do this for a week or two and see what happens. Small things may be enough to move the relationship in a positive direction. You can also use communal language, like *us* and *we*, which has been shown to lead to higher levels of commitment. When you talk to each other, say "*our* dog is making a mess" instead of "*your* dog is making a mess."

When you talk to other people, say, "*We* love Sunday brunch" instead of "*I* love Sunday brunch." Communal language can remind you and your partner that you're a team. Yes, you want external rewards, but what's important for commitment is the internal reward of caring for each other.

All the things we treasure about an activity or relationship help us be more committed. We are particularly influenced by intrinsic treasures: the things that make our activities inherently meaningful, fulfilling, and fun. Extrinsic treasures matter too, of course, particularly when they are fair relative to what others are getting.

Fair and Equitable Treasures

Imagine arriving at your place of work to discover that the offices are being refurbished and that for two weeks you are being relocated to temporary office space. Your secretary smiles and shows you to your new office. You look around. You notice that relative to your normal office, this one is dark and small and windowless. The next thing you realize is there are three small desks rather than one big one. You've been at the company fifteen years and you handle the most profitable contracts, so you wonder what's going on. You turn to ask your secretary, but she has gone quietly, as there is no office door to close. You try not to let it bother you. "It's temporary," you tell yourself. "We're all stuck in this situation together. Maybe it will feel better after coffee." You make your way to the break room, peeking in along the way at your coworkers, who seem to be adjusting to their new temporary situations.

There's Tasha, who's been with the company for two years. You learn she's in the same kind of sad office as you. There's Adam, who was hired the year after you. He doesn't have a window either, but at least he has an office to himself with a normal desk and *a flippin' door*. You walk down the hall and see Parker in his new office. The greenest on the team, he often relies on you, Ed, and Tasha for advice. He has a private office with a large mahogany desk and floor-to-ceiling windows! You look at him leaning back in his leather chair and taking in the view. He turns to see you, scrunches his nose, and lifts his shoulders apologetically.

You pour your weak cup of coffee and reluctantly trudge back to your dive of a shared closet. Your officemates, of varying levels of seniority, are now at their tiny desks and seem to be working. You sit down and stare at the 2008 calendar hanging on the wall that no one has bothered to remove and you think, "It's going to be a long two weeks."

This situation may sound absurd, but it was the setup of an inventive researcher who seized the opportunity to study the relationship between equity and feeling rewarded in the context of a real insurance company. The organization was undergoing a change in office space, and the researcher convinced the company to allocate the temporary offices at random, rather than by seniority. As such, some people received more than they deserved, given what they did for the company. Social scientists call this being *overbenefited*. Others received less than they deserved given their contributions, which social scientists call being *underbenefited*. There was also a control group, composed of employees who happened to be assigned to offices that fit their perceived status level, and thus they were neither over- nor underbenefited.

The researchers administered a series of surveys to discover how employees were impacted by the change. Halfway through the two-week period, employees rated how rewarding their job was, as they had done prior to the office switch. The people who were neither over- nor underbenefited felt as rewarded as they normally did, but for everyone else things were radically different. As expected, the overbenefited workers in the nicer offices felt significantly more rewarded and satisfied than the underbenefited people in their subpar offices. But job satisfaction and equitable rewards was only part of the story. The insurance company had existing data on job performance, measured primarily by the number of cases completed in a given period, and they continued to measure performance during the study period. Job performance and productivity among the underbenefited group declined significantly. And the overbenefited folks? Their job performance and productivity measurably increased. It's as if the groups adjusted their performance to fit the reward level of the office they received.

This pattern can be understood by what social scientists call Equity Theory. Equity Theory shows that satisfaction, a key part of commitment, comes not only from the raw amount of rewards we receive from a job or relationship but also from whether those rewards seem fair relative to what we put in and what others are getting. We have a social sensibility that says, if person A contributes more, she should receive more, and if person B contributes less, he should get less. Have you ever looked at someone and thought, "That guy has a cool job and a great salary. What's he so upset about?" What may be upsetting him is that he works ten hours a day while his coworker with the same job and the same salary takes three-hour lunch breaks to play *Left 4 Dead 2* on his computer. We are often less likely to treasure what we have—even if it's good—if it doesn't seem fair.

People don't let unfair rewards go without a response. One of the ways to respond is to leave the organization, and research supports this very chain of events:

feeling underbenefited → dissatisfaction → decreased commitment → turnover

Those who stay will try, consciously or not, to balance the inequity. They might work to restore *actual equity* by doing just what the folks at the insurance company did. The overbenefited group worked harder to justify their nicer offices, and the underbenefited group dropped their performance to compensate for their poorer ones. People also work to restore actual equity by speaking up and asking for change. Or they could start pilfering staplers and printer paper to compensate. Another option is to attempt to restore *psychological equity*. This requires a change not in behavior, but in perception. In this case, the underbenefited worker might think, "Well, I did miss that meeting last Tuesday, and I kind of dropped the ball on the Franklin account. Maybe I deserved this office downgrade." Similarly, the overbenefited worker might think, "You know, I'm kind of a star among the new hires. If anyone has a shot at rising through the ranks quickly, it's me. Management must be recognizing my potential." These rationalizations demonstrate how uncomfortable we are with inequitable rewards—when it becomes too much to bear we either modify our behavior (in this case by raising or lowering our output), do mental gymnastics to make the inequity seem fair, or reduce our commitment and consider leaving.

Relationship Equity

Equity issues show up in romantic relationships as well, but with a slight variation. Typically, people develop relationships with others whom they perceive to be their equals. For example, the *matching hypothesis* accurately predicts that partners will be about equivalent in physical attractiveness. I joke with my students, "Do you really want to know how attractive you are? Take a look at your partner." This is not always true, of course. Sometimes one person is quite a bit more physically attractive than the other, but the matching hypothesis accounts for this as well. If someone has more to offer in terms of looks, the other person likely balances the equation by offering rewards in another area, like status or earning potential. Take the classic 1973 study in which *Psychology Today* readers filled out questionnaires rating their own and their partner's attractiveness, along with other qualities like socioeconomic status and expressions of love and self-sacrifice. As predicted, the more physically attractive a person is relative to his partner, the more likely it is the partner offers a different treasure, such as a higher income or a self-sacrificing nature.

Clearly, partners need not contribute equally in every area, especially in a communal relationship. Each of us brings different skills and strengths. What's more important is the spirit of giving, in which both people contribute to the relationship in practical ways, like cleaning the floors or paying for the movie, and in emotional ways, like listening and touching, and they acknowledge the contributions the other makes. However, a long-term relationship will inevitably go through periods when one partner needs to carry more weight. Both people have to accept this fluctuation if the union is to remain stable. Partners can't contribute equally every single day, but if their contributions balance over time and there is a general spirit of fairness, their satisfaction will be greater.

An ongoing sense of inequity that never gets addressed can put the stability of a relationship at risk. Sometimes this is the result of a couple falling on hard times. Imagine a couple, Amanda and Jonathon, who equally contribute to their relationship. Amanda takes care of their twin boys, works part-time, and uses her earnings for groceries and household items. Jonathon works full-time, does fewer chores, and pays the mortgage. The couple is satisfied with this arrangement. They contribute to creating a good life for themselves and their family, and neither is unduly burdened. But then an economic crisis hits and Jonathon's division is shut down at work, leaving him without a job. In response, Amanda takes on more hours at work and starts paying the mortgage. Jonathon spends several hours a day looking for a new occupation. He offers to help care for the kids and do the housework, but since he's not in the habit of doing these things, and he's depressed and low on energy, Amanda is still taking care of those tasks too. Couples go through periods of imbalance like this all the time and stay intact. But a relationship that becomes an ongoing burden to one person must be addressed if it is to endure.

As in the workplace, there are three options to balance an unequal relationship. We can create balance by working to make an actual change. Perhaps Amanda starts a conversation: "Honey, I'm doing all the grocery shopping and caring for Ricky and Bobby, and I'm paying the mortgage. I'm getting stressed. Can we sit down and come up with a plan for getting through this?" This is where honest, effective communication is crucial (more about it in Chapter 4). For now, a helpful perspective is to see this is a relationship issue, rather than a "you are the problem" issue. We can also restore balance by making a psychological shift in the form of a rationalization. For example, when Jonathon notices things aren't quite equal, he thinks, "Yeah, she's doing all the housework and paying for the mortgage, but I pay her back with *my special love moves*." Amanda, of course, may have a different opinion on the matter. The last option, just like in the workplace, is that the underbenefited partner decides that this is no longer a good commitment and leaves the relationship. That decision would depend on the other elements that affect commitment as well.

How important is equity to commitment and the long-term viability of a relationship? Social psychology researcher Susan Sprecher tracked one hundred couples over five years. Every six months to a year, she surveyed both partners and asked them how "rewarding their partner's contributions have been" in terms of affection/warmth, status, money, material goods, services, and sex. They indicated how fair they thought their exchange was and the degree to which they were getting a "better or worse deal" than their partner. She recorded their satisfaction level in the relationship and their level of commitment. Sprecher compared each of these factors for the couples who broke up to those of the couples who stayed together. One finding about equity stands out: Relationships that ended were significantly more likely to have a woman who reported being underbenefited during the course of the relationship.

Most relationship researchers agree that women are at a greater risk than men of feeling underbenefited, at least in the Western world. The primary cause is an unequal distribution of housework and child care. A deeply rewarding aspect of a relationship is teamwork, shared responsibility, and reciprocity of kindness and support. If a couple can design a home system that feels fair to both partners over time, they will minimize feelings of inequity and can focus on the other rewards they experience together.

So far we know a few things about how treasures influence commitment. In general, the more we treasure something, the more attached we'll be to the source that provides it. In the contexts of work, exercise, and love, intrinsic treasures are particularly important. It's also helpful to create an environment that people perceive as generally fair so they can remain committed through occasional periods of inequity. Now for something you need to know if you want to use extrinsic treasures to build commitment: Extrinsic treasures pack a bigger punch when they're offered at random and surprising moments.

The Power of Random Treasures

I was having a rough day. Something unethical had emerged on a research team, and my efforts to rectify it had been met with resistance by a more powerful member. Distraught, I called my husband and explained what had happened. Despite the situation, I would attend my monthly girls' night out and see him afterward. While with friends, I tried very hard to be in the moment and not think of my concerns. It was difficult, and I found myself staring out the restaurant window. Just then, I saw my husband looking back as he drove by in his car. "He must be checking up on me, making sure I'm actually with girlfriends," I joked. A few minutes later, he walked inside and handed me a wrapped box. "I know it's been a long day. I thought you might like this." After a quick hello to my friends, he slipped out.

I opened the box and saw a coffee cup. It was a ceramic version of those paper cups you only get on the streets in New York City. Those blue and white ones that say, "We are happy to serve you," and have a rendering of a Greek vase on the side. I smiled. My husband knew that cup would bring back memories of coffee in one of the most wonderful cities in the world, and now I could drink out of it at any time. I treasure that cup, and I treasure the memory of his unpredictable actions that day.

So here's the question: Would I have treasured the cup as much if I had been expecting a gift? You might think we should or would value a particular reward in equal measure regardless of the circumstances under which we receive it. It's the same cup, after all, and we use it for the same purpose. But it turns out it doesn't typically work that way. What if it was given among the expected presents on Christmas? Or if I'd opened it on my birthday, thinking it would be a gold bracelet? Rewards tend to get more attention and feel more pleasurable when we cannot predict if or when they will come.

B. F. Skinner revealed this peculiarity when studying the behavior of rats. First he discovered what we consider self-evident today: If you want someone (say, a rat) to do something (like press a lever), give him a reward (maybe a chicken nugget). But Skinner noticed something else. Once the rat realized he could expect the reward and he was guaranteed to get it by pressing the lever, he lost some of his motivation. Then Skinner made his next discovery. The rat was more motivated when he received the nugget at random intervals, rather than every single time he pressed the lever. That is, sometimes he received it and sometimes he didn't, and he never knew when that would be. You might think the rat would lose interest with that kind of unpredictability, but the opposite was true. Not knowing when or how frequently the reward would come, the rat became more committed to stay by the lever and press it repeatedly. This same phenomenon happens with people.

Let's take an example of using the power of random reward to encourage commitment among people who are recovering from addiction. Some community clinics have experimented with randomly rewarding their outpatients for attending group therapy and passing a drug test. Those who show up for group counseling with a clean urine sample get to put their name in a bowl. A few names are drawn at random and those folks get to draw a prize. Most of the prizes are quite small, like a one-dollar McDonald's coupon (that will get you approximately two chicken nuggets). A few are moderate, like a ten-dollar movie ticket. One prize is always a jumbo item worth about a hundred dollars. Even with the prevalence of small rewards, the random chance of receiving a prize makes a significant impact on the behavior of those in treatment relative to those in standard outpatient care. They attend significantly more treatment days, remain in treatment longer, and achieve a longer period of drug abstinence.

The awareness of the power of random reward has implications at work, in relationships, and nearly everywhere else. Let's say you have a goal to assist others toward a higher level of commitment at work. If you want to increase the degree to which your employees treasure the rewards you provide, I suggest you be a little unpredictable. Don't announce in advance that whoever has the highest sales of the week will get a gift certificate to the local steakhouse. Instead, wait until the end of the week and without prior notification give the top salesperson the gift certificate, or tickets to a music or sporting event. You can also do things that don't cost any money. You can acknowledge a top employee in a public way, like on a social networking site, or privately by writing a personal thank-you note. You can do something creative, like naming a food item in the cafeteria after them: Beth's Beef Burrito or Po-Boy Patrick.

Now, I'm not suggesting you should offer incentives only at unpredictable moments. People need a baseline of expected compensation to keep coming back. But after that baseline has been met and one feels generally satisfied with the job, product, or service, it's a good time to layer on random treasures that increase interest and commitment.

Unexpected treasures can help increase what we value in a romantic relationship as well. Every now and then, think about giving something extra for no good reason. Make a special dinner on an average Tuesday night. Compliment your darling's appearance, not on Saturday evening, but on a Monday morning. Complete an annoying task that will benefit your partner before you're asked to. Chances are, these unexpected acts will add up and become little treasures that are greatly appreciated.

The Flip Side of Random Treasures

From recovery to relationships, unexpected treasures can increase how much we value an activity, and this knowledge can be helpful if you have a commitment goal of assisting others. You can help others feel motivated, appreciated, and committed by layering baseline rewards with unexpected extras. But now for the downside. The power of intermittent rewards can keep you stuck in a commitment that no longer reflects what you want.

Let's say your goal is to move on from a relationship that isn't right. If you are having a hard time letting go, you might want to ask yourself whether this is due to getting something you treasure on a random and inconsistent basis. It's possible to end up committed to something or someone not because it's highly satisfying and serving you well, but because you've become like Skinner's rat, pounding the lever and hoping for a reward. When treasures come unexpectedly and infrequently you may find yourself *more* attached than if the treasures were consistent.

This appears to be an acute risk in abusive partnerships. Along with the pain, disappointment, and fear in such a relationship, there are random moments when the hurtful person is incredibly caring or giving. Because we never know when that kindness will come, we end up overvaluing it and looking past all the destructive actions. An extreme example occurs in Stockholm syndrome. This is the name for the experience hostages have when they develop an attachment to their abusive captor, leading them to defend the perpetrator and sometimes reject assistance from law enforcement. The hostage develops a bond with her perpetrator in part because of the unexpected moments of goodness and mercy in the midst of isolation and abuse.

If you are staying in a bad situation at work, in a relationship, or with a group of friends, carefully evaluate the circumstances. Consider whether you might be overvaluing the inconsistent, rare treasures while overlooking the damage or negative impact of staying. Notice if you are getting just enough reinforcement to remain committed, even though you know this is not the right path for you.

The power of random treasures can also be a liability when you wish to maintain a commitment. There may be a lot of good in your relationship or job, but perhaps you've stopped appreciating it because it's so consistent. One way to outsmart this tendency is to consciously value every treasure in your life, even the expected ones. You know your brain is going to give more credit to the unexpected, and that's okay, but don't let it take over. When that paycheck arrives, really look at it and count your blessings. A lot of good people aren't receiving paychecks. When you get that routine kiss or "I love you," take a moment to appreciate the gesture and what it means to you. Condition yourself to pay attention to the great things that you consistently get from your job, relationship, or hobby.

Clearly, not all rewards impact commitment equally. We particularly treasure those that are intrinsic, fair, unexpected, and, as you are about to see, unique.

The Power of Unique Treasures

Employees of Ben and Jerry's ice cream in Vermont get to take home free pints of the cold and creamy stuff every day. This is not a traditional perk. Like random rewards, *unique* rewards also influence commitment. We'll be more attached to something—whether a relationship, brand, or job—if it offers treasures the others don't.

Some organizations provide employees with experiences and benefits that would be hard to find anywhere else. They create a niche, identify their purpose, or do something unique and then share it with their employees. When people work for companies that provide unique and treasured benefits, they are less likely to go anywhere else, even with the promise of a bigger paycheck.

Ben and Jerry found their niche long ago. These two men were committed to great ice cream, but also to having a low impact on the environment, even before "green" was cool. Their company has long used energy-efficient technology at their manufacturing plants. They send dairy waste back to their supply farms, where it's transformed into methane to power the farm. They are piloting a highly efficient "cleaner, greener" freezer to store their ice cream. It's no wonder people employed by Ben and Jerry's feel good about their work. They treasure their affiliation with a company that is dedicated to a cleaner environment. And at the end of a long workday, they get to celebrate with a pint of Chunky Monkey or Karamel Sutra.

Starbucks is another organizational standout, for a number of reasons. One is the compensation package offered to its employees. This package, called Your Special Blend, consists of a variety of benefits from which employees pick to meet their particular needs. One person might choose the adoption assistance, paid time off, and support for elder care. Another might select emergency financial aid, the retirement plan, and domestic partner benefits. There are many options, allowing employees to choose the right "blend" of benefits. With a customizable package like this, it's no wonder Starbucks was recently listed on the Fortune 100 Best Companies to Work For.

This is all good news if your goal is to increase commitment in others. If you can identify what you uniquely offer and then give it generously, it increases the chances that others will want to stick around. The power of unique treasures can be bad news, however, if your goal is to let go of a commitment. Sometimes you can be seduced into thinking that the treasures you're receiving are so unique they can't be found elsewhere, and this can lead you to stay committed to a decision that is less than ideal. Margaret, for example, had a psychological attachment to the home where she had raised her children. Her husband had passed away and the home was too large to care for, but she couldn't bear to leave the house because of its unique treasures, namely the memories it held. Margaret's children, now grown, married, and starting their own families, begged her to downsize, but she wouldn't budge. She didn't want to let go of what was so special about her house, those irreplaceable memories.

But the truth is many treasures, even the ones that appear to be unique, can be found in alternative situations that better suit your needs. This requires being open to other options, and putting in the effort to pursue them. In Margaret's case, one day she visited a friend who had moved into a patio home near a city park. The two friends sat outside on the deck, conversing, sipping tea, and watching children play in the park. As Margaret watched the children, it stirred fond memories of her own children when they were young. It started to dawn on her that her home wasn't the only source of family memories. Memories can be stimulated by many things, like old photographs or children playing in a park. For the first time she considered living somewhere else, perhaps here, in the same neighborhood as one of her closest friends. She envisioned her grandchildren enjoying the park and creating new memories. Realizing that what she treasured about her home could be developed elsewhere, Margaret finally let go and put her house up for sale.

If you are stuck in an unfulfilling job or relationship because you think there is nothing better out there, it may be because you think you'll never find the same "unique" treasures again. When you're able to see that what you treasure can be found somewhere else, you can free yourself from the dependent part of commitment and make a positive choice. The action plan for letting go of a commitment can be found in Chapter 8.

It's Subjective: Get Their Perspective

While research tells us that rewards are more highly treasured—and lead to greater commitment—when they are intrinsic, fair, unexpected, and unique, studies can't tell us what any particular person will treasure. The experience of treasuring something is highly subjective. So if you aim to increase commitment in another person or group, it's important to discover what is rewarding *from their perspective*. This requires asking, listening, and observing, rather than assuming that others will treasure the same things you do.

Think about romantic relationships, for instance. Early in our relationship, I assumed my husband would treasure verbal expressions of love and affection, as they were highly valued in my family growing up. After observing his behavior over time, however, I realized that habitual verbal expressions aren't what he values most. To him they're just words and do relatively little to bolster commitment. Gary Chapman's popular book, *The Five Love Languages*, is a helpful resource that explains that different people are rewarded by different types of behaviors in romantic relationships. He says there are five primary ways of expressing love, and one of these ways will resonate with your partner more than the others. The trick is to understand your partner's "love language" and realize it might be different from your own. While some intuitively based relationship books bear little resemblance to the findings in academic research, Chapman's love languages have been tested by communication scholars and found to be valid. The five categories of loving behaviors are: providing affirmations (verbal expressions of love), spending quality time (doing activities as a couple), giving gifts (like New York coffee cup replicas), acts of service (completing your honey-do's), and physical touch (caressing and more). Think for a moment about which of these categories would most communicate love to you. Is it possible that your partner is trying to reward you in his own way, and you aren't experiencing it because it's in a different love language? If so, is there a way to talk about it?

It's important to understand what's rewarding from others' perspective in the workplace as well. If you attempt to reward your employees with fantastic company parties when what they want is updated computers that increase efficiency, you have done little to increase their level of commitment. It's better to determine what your people value, as did one government agency. They surveyed their employees and asked: If you could have anything to make the workplace more rewarding, what would it be? They expected to hear about salary increases and espresso machines. Instead, the employees identified two things that were completely unanticipated. First, they wanted to spend an hour or so with the commissioner to get a firsthand look at what goes on in his office. Second, they wanted to switch positions with another employee for half a day. As it turns out, they wanted to see things from someone else's point of view because they thought it would improve how they did their jobs—nothing to do with espresso at all. If you ask, listen, and observe, you can discover what's rewarding from the other person's point of view, and that's what will affect his or her commitment.

Moving Forward

Treasures are the aspects of a relationship or activity that you deeply value. That value is based on a number of things, such as rewards that are intrinsic, equitable, unexpected, and unique. Treasures are a large part of whether you are satisfied with a commitment, and a high level of satisfaction predicts you'll stick with it. If you can't do anything about the treasures in your situation, however, don't worry. There are three other elements to investigate—troubles, contributions, and choices—and change in any one of the elements can change the whole equation.

The Takeaway
Using Knowledge of Treasures to Affect Your Commitment Goals

All In

If you are interested in going all in, you will benefit from increasing your treasures. Consider one or more of the following avenues for doing so.

- Look for and develop your intrinsic treasures, the feeling you get inside from participating in something meaningful.

- Proactively create the treasures that will mean the most to you.

- Accept times of inequality, and engage in healthy dialogue to ask for what you need to balance out an ongoing sense of unfairness.

- Value new and unexpected rewards, but also remember to treasure the predictable ones.

- Identify what's unique about the job, activity, or person that is important to you.

- Let others know in a positive way what you treasure, so they can take your perspective.

Moving On

If you are interested in moving on, take a fresh and honest look at your treasures. Consider one or more of the following avenues for starting the process of de-committing.

- Be honest about whether you are able to create meaningful intrinsic treasures in the current commitment.

- Proactively look for other options that include the treasures that mean the most to you.

- Stop overvaluing the random, intermittent treasures. See the whole picture.

- Identify what is unique about you that can be applied to people and situations beyond this commitment.

- Stop overvaluing future treasures that may never come. Realistically assess the treasures available now. If nothing were to change, would you stay?

Assisting Others

If you are interested in assisting others toward greater commitment, it helps to increase their treasures. Consider one or more of the following avenues for doing so.

- Help people develop intrinsic treasures. In work that means emphasizing tasks that are important and complex, and in sport and exercise that means providing experiences that are enjoyable and connecting.

- Be aware that people judge rewards on whether they are perceived to be fair. Do your best to develop an environment in which people contribute equally, or in which high contributors gain greater rewards.

- In addition to predictable benefits, offer random treasures that surprise, inspire, and motivate.

- Develop what is unique about you, and share that uniqueness with others.

- Take others' perspective. Don't assume you know what other people will treasure, but work to see treasures from their point of view.

▪ CHAPTER 4 ▪

Troubles: What's Holding You Back?

(Treasures – Troubles) + Contributions – Choices = Level of Commitment

IT is estimated that nearly half of all Americans will drop out of their church. Others will question their beliefs at some point in their lives, and wonder whether they should continue with the spiritual or religious practices inherited from their family. While the trend to temporarily or permanently leave the church is strongest during adolescence, my graduate student Kristine Bingham took a leave of absence in her thirties.

Kristine was devoted to her faith. It was the greatest part of her life and identity, and it guided her perspective of the world. Because her religion taught total devotion to God and church, she took a series of oaths to increase her commitment to the church and its principles. The most important of these oaths was to marry and never divorce. This was a mandate, but it was also what Kristine wanted.

She was so dedicated to her way of life as taught by her religion that even though she knew her husband was gay before they were married, she believed that with the right effort and devotion she could make her marriage work. Despite the couple's best efforts, however, the complexities of the marriage were unmanageable. The pain of being in an unhappy marriage, which her religious commitment wouldn't allow her to leave, led Kristine to ask some difficult questions about her faith.

"I started to wonder why the only two options were to remain in a terrible marriage or go to hell. Why did the thing that I was told I wanted most and that would bring me the most happiness—being married forever—feel like a death sentence? Knowing my impossible choice, and feeling like my needs didn't matter, felt suffocating. None of it made sense. I was terrified that if I didn't want what I had always believed I wanted (and been told I wanted), I was a bad person. But I knew that wasn't true. I was a good person. And I wanted good things. For me, for my husband, and for my children."

The process of reconsidering her marriage and her religion was heart wrenching. Ultimately, however, the internal struggle allowed her to leave a harmful commitment and reengage with her husband and church in a different way.

"There was nothing more important to me than pleasing God, and that included my commitment to my marriage. To walk away ripped my life apart. But then I did it, and incredibly everything was okay. Nothing fell apart. I just took a deep breath and said to myself, 'All right . . . Oh look . . . I'm not dead. Everything is going to be okay.' Not only did it not destroy me; my life is now better than I ever imagined. It was an ugly marriage but a beautiful divorce, definitely the best thing for me, for my former husband, and for our two children."

Today, Kristine appears more committed to her family than

ever before, if in a different way. "I'm committed to my ex-husband as friends and as co-parents. When I wasn't so worried about having the perfect family and getting to heaven, I realized that I just wanted what's best for my children. I wanted to get along with my ex-husband because that would be best for us all. And I'm a better parent now than when I was burdened with the guilt of thinking I was evil. How could it be evil to want good things for everyone?"

She's also found a new way to exist within her religion. At first she thought she'd have to abandon it completely, including the aspects she loved and that are deeply a part of her. But during a period of separation she realized she could commit on her own terms.

"I had to make the decision to walk away, create some space for myself, and then choose. There are things about my faith that I really cherish, and I am committed to living those things. Like treating others with dignity. . . . It is something I want to do innately, not because it's a mandate.

"Today I teach a class for people who are new to the religion. There's a manual that tells me what to say, but when I teach my class, instead of preaching, I ask a lot of questions. I ask people what they think, because that's what I asked myself. I don't teach anything I don't personally believe, and if I don't know something, I say so. This time around it's about what is happening in the present moment where I try to create positive, enriching experiences person to person.

"That's my religion now. I do it my own way."

The Meaning of Troubles

Kristine's story reveals an inner conflict many of us have experienced. Sometimes there's a commitment in your life you deeply value, and yet something about it feels wrong. Being in this place can be painful. At the same time, the inner conflict may be an important part of your growth, an opportunity to reexamine what you value and make positive changes. In the end you may choose to walk away and seek something new, or, depending on the circumstances, you may choose a path of deeper commitment.

In the previous chapter we talked about treasures, the things you find fulfilling that increase the chance you'll stay. In this chapter we investigate *troubles*—the things you find unfulfilling or costly that increase the chance you'll leave a job or relationship, or quit a long-term goal. Recall that satisfaction is a key predictor of commitment, and your level of satisfaction is based on the degree to which treasures outweigh troubles. In some workplaces, for example, the troubles will be too great compared to what you gain, and your commitment level will remain low. In other cases, there will be so much you treasure about the job that you're willing to put up with a significant amount of troubles. And sometimes you'll find you're highly committed despite low levels of satisfaction, likely because you've invested a lot in that job or you're unaware of your other choices—elements we'll discuss in Chapters 5 and 6. In this chapter we'll focus on why and how troubles impact your level of satisfaction and commitment.

Troubles vary in severity and acceptability. Some troubles associated with a commitment are simply the cost of admission—a small price to pay to achieve meaningful goals. Troubles that come with getting a college degree, for example, may be the long hours of study, the unpleasant part-time job that helps cover your tuition, and sharing a shoe box apartment with two crazy roommates. These may be acceptable costs to you because a commitment to education takes you closer to the kind of life you want to live. In other cases, troubles are significant and personally damaging. They limit your potential and keep you from achieving what you want most in your life. These troubles might include a supervisor who sees you as competition and devises ways to hold you back, constant criticism from a spouse, leading you to feel like a failure, or witnessing unethical behavior on a team. Troubles like these lead you to ask important questions: Can I put these problems into perspective and focus on the valuable parts of the commitment? Is there a way to minimize troubles, and is my goal worth it if I can't? Is there another choice that would bring me closer to the life I really want?

Some troubles are apparent from the beginning. They show up on that bad first date or that miserable first week on the job. You may decide right there and then that this isn't the person or place for you. In other cases, you'll give it some time to discover whether the good parts of being with this partner will outweigh the bad. After being married for six years, my husband confided that he'd seen a red flag on our third date. Apparently, I sometimes swig my drink out of the side of my mouth in a way that makes me look psychopathic. Thank goodness he decided to overlook that and give us a chance.

Other troubles emerge over time. After two years of courting potential investors, you still don't have the capital to launch your product. After three years of playing hockey in the "fifty and older" league, and two tailbone injuries, you discover your body doesn't heal as quickly as it used to and you're not so young anymore.

After ten years working at the same job, you realize the stress of the position is damaging your mental and physical health. These are troubles you didn't expect when you signed on. Since commitment is about our level of psychological attachment to something and our intention to continue, troubles can temporarily or permanently call our attachment and intention into question. Sometimes that's appropriate, like when you're committed to people and activities that aren't in your best interest. Other times a drop in commitment is unfortunate, particularly when the activity adds value to your life. In that case, you'll want to consider whether there's a way to minimize the troubles.

Here's what we know about the interaction between troubles, satisfaction, and commitment:

1. Unfortunately, troubles affect us more deeply than treasures do.
2. Treasures must outnumber troubles by about five to one to maintain satisfaction and commitment.
3. Sometimes we create our own troubles by how we interpret events.
4. Some of the ways we respond to troubles will reduce commitment, and some will increase commitment.

If you want to go all in or assist others to higher commitment, this chapter will help you identify ways to reduce the negative impact of troubles on commitment. If your goal is to reduce your commitment level to something in your life, you'll have the opportunity to reflect on the reasons this commitment is so troubling, and learn what steps can make it easier to let go. Let's begin with why troubles tend to impact us more than treasures.

Bad Apples and the Negativity Bias

Eliza Byington was a PhD student at the University of Washington Foster School of Business when she observed an interesting phenomenon in her workplace. As a general rule, her coworkers didn't work as a team. They avoided one another, in and out of work, and were hesitant to share information. But things radically changed when one of the group's members took a medical leave of absence. Without the presence of this particular person, the group behaved quite differently. They began helping each other, sharing information, and spending time together after the workday was over. Both work productivity and enjoyment increased. After a few weeks, the culprit returned from his medical leave and—you guessed it—the work climate reverted to its previous state. Byington was amazed at how much influence this one negative person had on nearly everyone in her workplace. Curious, she and her husband, Will Felps, also a PhD student, began reading research literature on the topic. Most of what they read didn't correspond with her observation. Instead, the literature suggested that one difficult member would be brought back in line by the power of the group. So what could account for what Byington encountered?

Difficult people in the workplace have gone by many names: poor performers, team destroyers, and bad apples. These are people with a negative attitude, who violate norms of equity and engage in inappropriate social behavior. Bad apples are poor organizational citizens, and their behavior has a large impact on the groups they are involved with.

Felps decided to investigate the influence of three kinds of bad apples on small groups for his dissertation. On the National Public Radio show *This American Life*, he referred to these bad apples as

the Jerk, the Slacker, and the Depressive Pessimist. He hypothe-
sized that each of these would harm the team environment and the
group's productivity. To test his hypothesis he enlisted a confeder-
ate who would take on the role of the bad organizational citizen in
an experimental group setting. Felps found Nick, an actor who
would play the part to perfection. Experimental participants were
assigned to teams of four, where they engaged in a management
task. To provide motivation, they were informed that the best per-
forming team would get a one-hundred-dollar prize. Nick was
sometimes a member of the four-person group, with the other
participants unaware that he was a plant.

This was when the experiment (and fun) began. In some of the
groups, Nick played the Jerk. In this role, he attacked and insulted
people as they attempted to work on the task, making comments
like, "Are you kidding me?" and "Have you actually taken a business class before?" He regularly shot down ideas and offered no
constructive solutions of his own. In other groups, Nick played the
Slacker by displaying a lack of involvement and effort. He leaned
back in his chair, put his feet on the desk, and occupied himself
with an unrelated task. This time, his comments consisted of
"Whatever" and "I don't care." In the third set of groups, Nick's
role was the Depressive Pessimist, in which he displayed both negativity and lack of motivation. During the group interaction, he
laid his head on the table and looked despondent. (To get himself
in the frame of mind of the Depressive Pessimist, Nick imagined
his cat had just died.) His comments were centered on the team's
likely failure and his disinterest in participating. Finally, some
groups were fortunate and consisted of four real participants, without the influence of Nick.

Felps found that bad apples have a profound effect on small

groups. Teams that included Nick in one of his roles performed 30 to 40 percent worse than teams without a bad apple. According to Felps, this may be because groups with a bad apple tended to fight more and share information less. In addition, when he watched the video recordings of the group interactions, he noticed that team members typically took on the characteristics of the bad organizational citizen. When Nick was the Jerk, the other group members became abrasive as well, and not just to Nick, but to each other. When he was the Slacker, other members of the group started emulating his lazy attitude, saying things like, "Let's just do whatever." And with Nick as the Depressive Pessimist, Felps noticed that by the end of the forty-five-minute task many of the participants had laid their own heads on the table. Felps's research supports an old cliché: One bad apple can indeed spoil the bunch.

This study is one example of what social scientists have found again and again: Negativity is more powerful than positivity. I realize these findings are initially disappointing, but bear with me. Understanding this phenomenon is crucial to dealing with the negative elements that can affect the level of commitment in yourself and others. In the early 2000s, two teams of scholars pointed out that many psychological studies show bad experiences have a more pronounced and durable effect than equivalent good experiences. One group of authors, led by Roy Baumeister, of Florida State University, included the following study findings as examples: First impressions of a person are impacted more by negative information than by positive information; the intensity of our disappointment over losing a sum of money tends to outweigh the amount of happiness we experience upon gaining an equivalent sum of money; one bad sexual experience affects us more, and for a longer period of time, than one great sexual experience; and, as you might expect, undesirable events influence our daily mood more than desirable events. A team of authors from the University of Pennsylvania agreed. They saw this tendency as such a prominent feature of being human that they dubbed it the *negativity bias*.

Why are we biased toward negativity? Why do troubles influence us more deeply, and for a longer period of time, than treasures? One possible explanation is that negative aspects of a job, relationship, or project require more cognitive effort. You have to evaluate how harmful the negative event is likely to be, what aspects of your life might be impacted, and how you might need to respond. Additionally, you must use cognitive effort to think optimistically about the negative event so it doesn't impact you more than necessary. Positive events, by comparison, require minimal processing. For example, let's say your girlfriend not only remembers and celebrates your birthday, but she buys you concert tickets to see your favorite rock band. This will be something you'll treasure; it will lift your mood immediately and perhaps become a fond memory. If, however, she not only forgets your birthday, but actually makes plans to go to the concert with her old high school boyfriend that night, not only will that dampen your immediate mood, it will likely make you question the whole relationship. You'll want to figure out why she would do that and how you should respond. Far more cognitive effort will be used and for a longer period of time.

Negative information may also be more powerful because it prompts you to consider making a change, whereas positive information does not. Say you're at work and your supervisor acknowledges you for three things at which you excel. No need for change there. But she also tells you one thing she's concerned about: You've been treating customers curtly at the end of the workday. Her one negative comment will take far more of your energy and attention because it requires you to think about changing. You'll likely ponder whether what she said is true, and if so why that might be. Perhaps you've been short with customers at the end of the day because you feel rushed to finish your tasks and get out the door. (The people at daycare get upset when you're even a few minutes late to pick up your son.) Has the pressure of the daycare's strict 5:15 deadline influenced the way you handle customers who come at 4:45? If so, what can you do about it? Perhaps you should find a new daycare. Perhaps you should discuss the problem with your boss. Perhaps you should figure out how to be more patient. Now you try to think of the three things the boss complimented you on, but you can't seem to remember what they are. You can't remember because the positive comments are being overshadowed by the negative comment requiring you to make a change.

An important caveat to the power of negativity is that while an event may be troubling in the moment, if the situation is resolved and there's a happy ending, that ending is what typically remains in our long-term memory. According to Daniel Kahneman, emeritus professor of psychology at Princeton University, we have two selves, the *experiencing self* and the *remembering self.* The way we experience something in the moment isn't the same as the way we remember it long term, because the ending is what we often take with us. Kahneman discovered this by asking research participants to hold one hand in a vessel of cold water. Some left their hand in water at fourteen degrees Celsius for sixty seconds (this is quite painful).

Some were required to leave their hand in for an additional thirty seconds, during which time the temperature was gradually increased by one degree. Those in the latter group rated the experience as less painful than those who experienced no increase in temperature, even though they had their hands in the cold water for a longer period of time. The main difference for the latter group was a slightly less painful ending experience.

This finding makes me think about people who commit to a difficult long-term goal, like training for and completing a marathon for the first time. During the process, runners will experience troubles like getting up early and enduring the physical discomfort of cold weather and exhaustive training. But what do these folks remember about their experience? If it ends well, they are likely to remember how meaningful it was to finish the marathon. The training was merely the price of admission, and it's this memory of the ending that encourages them to do it again.

If you're facing a troubling situation that's keeping you from a commitment goal, ask yourself this question: Is experiencing a rewarding conclusion worth the troubles along the way? If the satisfaction of completing your first marathon, first book, or new product is something you know you will treasure, then the troubles along the way will seem like a small price to pay. Keeping the prize in sight and consciously focusing on what you treasure about your commitment will help you to manage the difficulties along the way, and the happy ending will reinforce your level of commitment even in the face of significant troubles.

Given that troubles impact us more than treasures, we clearly need more treasures than troubles to be satisfied and committed. But the question is, how much more?

Balancing Treasures and Troubles

My interest in social science evidently began in the third grade. My best friend Molly's father was Robyn Dawes, a distinguished psychology researcher and department head at the University of Oregon. Dawes and a colleague had just written an article titled "Linear Prediction of Marital Happiness." Of course, I had not read the article. All I knew about it was what Molly had told me: *As long as you have sex more often than you fight, you'll be happy.*

Perhaps because my parents had recently divorced, I pondered Molly's explanation of her father's findings. My eight-year-old mind remained unconvinced—how could it be that simple? Years later, when I read Dawes's article, I saw that Molly had correctly conveyed her father's research. The authors asked couples to monitor their daily arguments and their daily sexual intercourse for more than a month. The "rate of sexual intercourse minus rate of arguments" significantly predicted a couple's level of happiness. Further, the greater the margin of sex to arguments, the happier the couple professed to be. We can't say having more sex than arguments will *cause* you to be happier in your relationship, although it might. Happy people may simply fight less and have more sex. But the strong correlation points to an important truth: In order for us to be happy with a commitment, our treasures can't be equal to our troubles. They must *outweigh* troubles. In-depth studies on satisfaction and commitment in love and work provide a consistent answer to the question of how many treasures are needed to balance a trouble.

Let's Talk About Relationships

There you are, standing at the door of John Gottman's Love Lab with your partner. You've heard that Gottman can predict whether a couple will stay together or divorce with over 90 percent accuracy. No, he isn't a psychic. He's a researcher who has meticulously observed and analyzed thousands of couples for more than forty years. With degrees in mathematics and psychology, he uses rigorous scientific measures to determine the elements of marital interaction that predict a stable or unstable union.

In the lab, you and your partner go through a series of activities. First, you individually fill out a questionnaire about how happy you are in the relationship. Then, together you share your history as a couple during a recorded interview. Next, you are asked to select a topic for discussion that has historically caused the two of you trouble. Once you've picked your topic, you're attached to a battery of physical monitors. One is for your heart rate. One is to measure sweat. Your chair is outfitted with a mechanism that measures fidgeting. (You overhear the lab assistant call it the "jig-o-lometer.") Now it's time to begin discussing the problem area. Since you know the conversation is being recorded, you try to be calm and as tactful as possible with your responses. But as the memory of this ongoing conflict comes back to you, you can't force your body to ignore what it feels. You forget you're in a lab and the conflict proceeds as it often does at home. You might roll your eyes and interrupt, or tell your partner you understand. Soon the time is up and the monitors are removed from your body. You know the recording will be coded for specific verbal and nonverbal expressions. Positive expressions include showing interest, being empathetic, and providing affection. Negative expressions include criticism, anger, and hostility. Dr. Gottman meets with you to discuss what he saw in your tape. Years later, he'll ask if you're still married, and your response data will be plugged into a database and used to advance our knowledge about the factors that create a stable marriage.

The Love Lab procedure has allowed Gottman to predict divorce with incredible accuracy, based on just a few key indicators. One of those is the balance of positivity to negativity in a couple's interaction. Couples in marriages that last have *five times* the number of positive expressions to negative expressions. In marriages that end, there is an almost equal number of positive to negative expressions, with just a bit more negative. It's not the actual number of positive or negative remarks that matters; it's the *ratio* of positive to negative that counts. Couples who have high levels of negative expression can survive as long as they balance it with five times as much positive expression. A couple with very little emotional expression can also be in a stable relationship. Maybe they don't display a lot of feeling, but as long as the balance is five to one, the relationship tends to succeed.

Given this information, it's fair to conclude the following: Because negative interactions harm relationships more than positive interactions uplift them—at a rate of five to one—it's essential to fill our committed relationships with many expressions of love, support, and encouragement to balance inevitable times of disagreement and hurt feelings. Every positive action counts, including small things like a touch on the arm, a casual compliment, or bringing home a little surprise. Day-to-day interactions, and not grand gestures, seem to matter most.

The workplace is a different environment, but as you'll see, the five-to-one phenomenon exists there as well.

Let's Talk About Work

Imagine you are an employee at a midsize company where your coworkers consist of engineers, information service technicians, and customer service reps. You and about fifty of your coworkers are randomly selected by a team of management researchers to participate in a study. They tell you to carry a little handheld computer, and at varying intervals the computer will beep and pose questions to you about your mood and what is happening in your work environment.

Before you get to work on day one of the study, you hear the first beep. You're asked how you are feeling this morning. You indicate the degree to which you feel a pleasant emotion like *pleased* or *satisfied*, and the degree to which you feel an unpleasant emotion like *blue* or *unhappy*. Your response will tell the researchers your *baseline mood* for the day—the place you start before arriving at work. Perhaps this morning you are slightly unhappy. You're still thinking about something annoying that happened yesterday, and you may have to manage it again today.

Once you're at work, a respected coworker pulls you aside and tells you she supports your new product idea. Your beeper goes off and you are asked to indicate whether a pleasant or unpleasant event has occurred at work. You report that a pleasant event has occurred with a coworker. You are asked about your mood, like you were earlier this morning, and you indicate that you are feeling moderately happy.

After lunch you are handling a service call over the phone. You are simply explaining how the product works when the customer becomes irate. He hasn't even attempted the instructions you provided and is claiming your company's product is faulty.

He calls you incompetent and demands to speak with your supervisor. You oblige. After you hang up the phone, you take a few deep breaths and remind yourself that everyone has to deal with personalities like this. Then, your handheld beeps and asks what has happened since the last beep—pleasant or unpleasant—and how you feel.

The researchers of this study, headed by Andrew Miner at the University of Minnesota, wanted to understand how much negative events at work impact our mood relative to positive events. Analyzing multiple reports over a ten-day-plus period, Miner found that the negative experiences influenced mood more than the positive ones. How much more? This should sound familiar: Negative events affected mood five times as much as positive events.

They also discovered what happens to our mood when both a positive and negative interaction occur within a short period of time. Let's say that within an hour we received both the angry customer call and support from our coworker, and were then asked to report on our mood. In this case, our mood would be more impacted by the unpleasant service call than by the coworker's praise. In fact, the positive event would do little to mitigate the impact of the negative, and our mood would drop as much as if only the negative event had occurred.

But the study did reveal something hopeful. The researchers found that when an employee started the day in a positive frame of mind, his mood got a bigger boost by pleasant events than if he'd started out less happy. Further, employees who started the day in a good mood were a little less impacted by negative events with coworkers. This tells us something about getting in the right frame of mind before heading to work. A preexisting positive state adds a little buffer to the troubles that come our way and enhances our appreciation of positive events when they occur.

If you have a commitment goal of assisting others, it's important to understand how powerful troubles are. In the workplace, even one bad apple or frustrating policy can significantly reduce the satisfaction and commitment of the group. The best remedy, of course, is to identify such troubling aspects (maybe the terribly outdated reimbursement process, or the bad apple who is creating a hostile work environment) and make it a priority to change those areas. But if that's not possible, you also might be able to overcome the problem by bringing a rich supply of positivity into the workplace to balance out the negative. If you have a commitment goal to go all in, you too can consciously generate positive interactions to counteract the troubling times. One small thing you can do at the start of the day or the beginning of the project is get into an optimistic frame of mind. A positive baseline mood gives you a bit of a buffer against the inevitable hardships, and a greater appreciation for the things you treasure.

This positive baseline may also help you avoid reading too much into potential troubles and making them worse than they are.

Creating Our Own Troubles

Have you ever done something totally innocent—maybe you forgot a meeting because it wasn't on your calendar, or maybe you said something that came out wrong—and the other person became quite upset, more so than you'd expect given the circumstances? It's hard to watch someone create significant troubles out of relatively innocuous incidents. You want to say to him, "Wait, there is no reason to be upset over this! Really, this is a minor situation and it doesn't mean what you think it does. Everything is good." But it's too late. He's created a story in his head about what your behavior means, and now he seems convinced his story is true. It may appear that our troubles are external, and many times they are, but some troubles are made worse by our interpretation of events. There is much in our external environment we cannot control, but if we work to control what we can (i.e., how we respond to external events), we'll be in a better position to deal constructively with negative experiences when they occur, and this can significantly minimize their impact.

Years ago, I traveled to the island of Oahu with my boyfriend Jeff, who is now my husband. Although the trip was primarily for business purposes, we were hoping to enjoy a few days of sightseeing, dining, and hanging out on the beach. Instead, business consumed most of the available time, and for a new relationship it was an unglamorous trip. I hoped Jeff didn't regret bringing me along. On the flight home, he appeared unresponsive. He didn't smile, engage in conversation, or laugh at my witty jokes. Observing his behavior, I quickly came to the troubling conclusion that he was not happy with me or our relationship. Insecurity filled my head and I instinctively worked harder to earn his affection, making the situation more awkward. This could have been a long flight for both of us, but before my destructive thinking went too far, I remembered something I teach in my communication courses: There is a difference between facts and our interpretation of the facts. The stories we tell ourselves about the facts can exacerbate troubles or even manufacture them.

Most of us are not the objective observers we believe we are. We don't examine a situation and take in raw data like a computer.

Our brains take in the data and automatically interpret it in a way that makes sense from *our perspective.* This natural human tendency can be problematic when we act upon our interpretations as if they are truth. Part of the problem, according to the authors of the bestselling book *Crucial Conversations,* is that when an event occurs, we tell ourselves a story about the external facts so quickly we hardly notice it. Then we think we are acting on the truth, when we're actually reacting to an internal story. On the plane, I told myself the story that Jeff was no longer happy with me, and given that story, I felt hurt and defensive. If I had responded according to my initial interpretation by making a passive-aggressive comment like "Sorry I'm making you miserable," I would have taken a minor trouble and turned it into something more serious. It turns out we do this all the time in relationships, at work, and even with strangers. We tell ourselves a story so fast and instinctively, especially when the situation feels risky, that we don't realize we're acting on the story rather than on the facts.

Facts are specific, objective, and observable events that a movie camera could capture. They are data with no interpretation. Sometimes when we go back to the facts we can see that many alternative stories could be developed, some of which wouldn't be troubling. Let's go back to the plane and the facts. Jeff was subdued and quiet. He didn't smile, engage in conversation, or laugh at my jokes. These are things an objective movie camera would see. As I reviewed the facts, I pondered a few alternative stories that could account for his behavior. He could simply be tired. He could be disappointed with the outcome of the business meetings. He could be preoccupied with the work that lies waiting on his desk. As I considered these other stories, my body began to relax and my feelings of insecurity began to change to empathy. I looked out the window and decided to take a nap. Later on, Jeff told me he was simply disappointed with the trip and felt bad that he had dragged me with him.

An important story that you frequently tell yourself is the story of what caused another person's behavior. If your partner comes home late for dinner without calling, for example, you will quickly develop a story for what caused it. You may think he's not as eager to come home as he used to be, or he doesn't respect your efforts. Or you could decide that something important came up at work or he simply lost track of time. Notice that in all these stories, one fact is the same: Your partner came home late. But the story you decide to embrace strongly impacts your level of satisfaction in a relationship.

Two leading scholars who have researched this phenomenon are Frank Fincham, at Florida State University, and Thomas Bradbury, from UCLA. In one study, they asked married people to think about a current marital problem and give their story for why the problem had occurred. They also asked participants what their story would be if their spouse criticized something they did, didn't pay attention to what they were saying, or started spending more time without them. The researchers looked for specific qualities within these stories. The first thing they looked for was whether the story indicated the behavior was caused by something *external*, like the circumstances, or by something *internal*, like the spouse's character. If the story for your partner coming home late is that something important came up at work, this indicates you think the behavior was caused by external circumstances. But if the story is she doesn't respect other people's time, it means the problem is based on an internal quality. The second thing the researchers looked for was whether the story indicated the spouse's behavior was perceived to be *intentional* or *unintentional*. Intention is important because it drives the motivation for behavior. If the behavior is coming home late without calling, the question is, did the spouse do it deliberately or was it by accident? Your story might indicate he was motivated to come home on time, but he got distracted and was unintentionally late. But if your story is he came home late to get back at you for overspending last week, then you perceive he was intentionally late.

Fincham and Bradbury found that distressed couples tell different stories than happy couples do. In distressed relationships, men and women are more likely to tell stories that indicate the problem is due to an internal characteristic of their partner, and the act was done intentionally. For example, if a man's partner is not paying attention to what he is saying, his story might be "because she doesn't care how I feel." If a woman's partner is spending more and more time without her, her story might be "because he is no longer interested in me." These stories indicate the cause of the behavior is internal and the partner is behaving that way on purpose. Stories like these reinforce the distress the couple feels: They tell these stories, they feel distressed; they feel distressed, they tell these stories. It's a difficult loop to get out of, and one that requires questioning the stories and being open to new interpretations and dialogue.

People with high relationship satisfaction, on the other hand, are more likely to tell stories indicating the problem is due to external environmental causes and is unintentional. The stories from happy partners might be "she didn't hear me because she's preoccupied with making dinner," and "he's got so much on his plate right now, so time with me is short." These charitable stories tend to enhance the relationship.

Sometimes when you notice yourself telling a story, it's important to ask your spouse for clarification. When you do a perception check, it's helpful to start with the facts before going into your story. For example, you could say, "I notice you've come home late twice this week without calling. It seems like you are either really busy, or maybe there's a reason you'd rather not come home. What's going on?" Now you can work to understand what's happening from his point of view. But even when engaging in a perception check, continue to be mindful of your stories. If your spouse responds, "Oh, I keep losing track of time because of this big project," you may still tell yourself the story that he's doing it intentionally or because of a character flaw. If he's more vague and says, "Work stuff. I don't want to talk about it right now," you're left with only your story, which could range from the suspicious "he's keeping a secret from me" to the more charitable "he must be exhausted from whatever's going on at work."

You can't control many of the events in your life. You can't force your spouse to pay attention to you, or make your boss promote you, or prevent unexpected challenges. But if you want to be happy, and if you want to remain committed, it is helpful to be mindful of both the facts and the stories you create as you interpret those facts. Whether you decide something was done intentionally or unintentionally will greatly exacerbate or defuse your experience of the trouble. A charitable explanation story is a great place to start if you want to respond to troubles in a positive way.

Note: Some behavior is unacceptable regardless of the reason. If you are being abused at home or work, it's a serious trouble regardless of the circumstances causing it. No story is justification for abusive behavior. Seek help from counselors, human resources, or the police when appropriate.

Responding to Troubles

Thom and Layla had been together for about six months when she became dissatisfied with one of his habits. She knew he had been a smoker when he was younger, but he didn't smoke when they met. Three months into the relationship, however, he resumed the habit, saying it was temporary. Layla tried to be understanding and didn't tell Thom how much it bothered her. She prayed he'd be able to stop when the stress at work had passed, and she sent him positive thoughts.

Another trouble reared its head a few months later when Thom had yet another excuse for why Layla couldn't meet his parents. In all their time together, she hadn't been introduced to his family, or he to hers, because each time they had plans, Thom found a last-minute reason to bail. Layla decided to voice her concern. She told Thom how important it was to her for their families to meet. She pointed out that something always seemed to get in the way. Thom responded with the usual excuses.

Layla realized that while Thom promised to quit smoking and promised to introduce her to his family, neither of these things had happened. She started to wonder if anything would change. She asked herself whether she could accept the relationship as it was. Her heart sank when she realized she could not be happy with things the way they were. Layla began to shut down. She quit asking Thom about his family. She quit caring about whether he would stop smoking. She gave less attention and effort to the relationship. Still, she wasn't sure she wanted to end it. But as more time passed, she found herself secretly hoping he'd leave her. Eventually she suggested they see other people, part of her expecting this would upset him enough to break it off. Instead, he agreed to the new arrangement. Layla told her friends she was "available" and soon thereafter, one of them set her up. She dated both Thom and the new guy for about a month, and before much longer she felt ready to finally end things with Thom.

According to Caryl Rusbult, our commitment expert from Chapter 2, and her colleague, Dan Farrell, there are four broad categories of responses when it comes to dealing with dissatisfaction. They call these responses *loyalty*, *voice*, *neglect*, and *exit*. Layla experienced all four. She began with loyalty. *Loyalty* is considered a passive way to remain committed during times of dissatisfaction. It's when we wait for things to get better and keep a positive attitude, without taking any direct action. Layla showed loyalty when she didn't say anything about Thom's smoking and stayed optimistic that he would keep his word and quit again. When the troubles didn't pass, Layla turned to *voice*, an active strategy to create change. She communicated what was troubling her and tried to find a solution when she asked for what she wanted—to meet each other's families and to understand the real reason behind Thom's reluctance. Both loyalty and voice are associated with high levels of commitment. We typically use these strategies when we have higher levels of satisfaction and plan to remain in the relationship or on the job.

We sometimes think that if someone is voicing his dissatisfaction, it means he's not committed. But the research reveals a different story. When people speak up, they are attempting to do something about the troubles that threaten their satisfaction and commitment. That's a good sign. When commitment is low, they're more likely to remain quiet and use the next two strategies— neglect and exit.

Because the troubles in her relationship greatly surpassed

what she treasured about it, Layla's commitment began to fade, leading to the third response, neglect. *Neglect* is a passive strategy for dealing with dissatisfaction. It occurs when we give up on making things better. As Layla realized these troubles weren't going away and she wasn't willing to live with them, she began to allow the relationship to deteriorate by giving it little attention or energy.

Finally, Layla decided to exit. *Exit* is an active way to end a commitment. It consists of quitting, leaving, or searching for a new opportunity. Layla exited emotionally when she began dating her new man, and physically when she broke off the relationship. Not surprisingly, neglect and exit are associated with lower levels of commitment.

Using Neglect and Exit

With neglect or exit two things happen: Problems are less likely to be resolved, and your commitment is likely to decline even more. Sometimes this is appropriate, depending on your goal, so let's look at some conditions under which neglect and exit are good choices.

Condition #1: Your Investment Is Low.

Let's say you go to a new barber and he makes some off-color comments you find offensive. After the disappointing haircut, you decide not to go back. You haven't invested much; you don't know this person well or feel any obligation to continue being a customer. At this point it doesn't seem appropriate to engage in a conversation about your dissatisfaction and ask him to refrain from making such comments. There are many other barbers, and you can easily find someone else. In this case, exit is a reasonable and appropriate choice.

Condition #2: You Want Some Space to Make a Decision.
Imagine you've been operating a small business for a long time, but now you're not sure the industry is right for you. The "powers that be" have initiated substantial new regulations that slow you down and increase your costs. At the moment, your troubles outweigh your treasures, and you need some time to determine your next move. You might decide it's time to research other options. Instead of giving 100 percent to your business, you give 80 percent, so you have time to pursue potential alternatives. Perhaps you even take a brief leave of absence. During this time, you work to discover whether you can remain committed or whether you want to permanently exit. In this case, neglect is a good choice because it allows you to gain some helpful perspective.

Condition #3: You've Already Decided This Situation Isn't for You.
Sometimes you already know a job or project isn't right for you or is unlikely to work out, but you have a hard time letting go. Since neglect and exit tend to reduce commitment, strategically neglecting an activity can be a helpful way to begin reducing your attachment. Spending time away can help you realize you have other choices, as it did for Layla.

Using Voice and Loyalty

What if, on the other hand, you are highly committed to something and want to keep it that way? Voice is your option when you want to actively change a troubling situation. Loyalty is what you need for a difficulty that you want to accept and trust will pass. Even though these are high-commitment choices, it doesn't mean things will always go smoothly. Let's take a look at the most effective way to use these responses, starting with voice.

Voice

Some troubling situations change on their own, but other times you must speak up. The question is: How will you voice your concerns? When you're feeling dissatisfied, you may use your voice in a way that exacerbates the trouble. The challenge is to communicate in a way that gains the other person's attention and trust. To effectively voice your troubles, consider the other person's goals in addition to your own. In other words, instead of focusing only on what's important to you, discover what's important to the other person and see if you can connect your needs with hers. Most people are far more likely to respond to your needs if it benefits them as well, and especially if they believe you care about their interests. Let me share a story that illustrates how a committed person inadvertently used her voice in a way that intensified the trouble, and more important, how she turned it around.

Tia was temporarily relieved of her regular duties in order to pursue a special project. She told several of her team members about the new assignment, and they were excited for her and wished her well. However, one of the team's members, Jannie, had not been informed, and when she found out she became angry. At the next unit meeting, Jannie said that giving Tia "special treatment" was unacceptable. She questioned the supervisor's integrity for allowing one of the team members to get out of "real work." Jannie argued with the supervisor for some time, while Tia and the rest of her coworkers sat quietly. When the supervisor did not change his mind, Jannie said a few select words and walked out of the meeting.

Jannie had a lot invested in her job. The work she did was important to her. When something bothered her, she spoke up. But the way she did it in this case created a divide between her, her supervisor, and her coworkers. She didn't resolve the problem at hand and likely added new troubles.

When we decide to voice our dissatisfaction, it can be tempting to take an approach similar to Jannie's. Troubles often bring up fears. Fears that others don't value us, don't understand us, or won't meet our needs. When fear shows up as frustration toward others, it can lead to harmful communication strategies that create even bigger troubles. So how can we use our voice in a way that increases the likelihood a solution will be found?

Conflict subsides when we use a problem-solving communication style that integrates the needs of both parties. Before speaking up, it's helpful to become clear about your own goals and the goals of others, and then communicate in a way that takes both into consideration. In Jannie's case, after the meeting, when her emotions had subsided, she reflected on her negative comments and tried to get at the heart of what was bothering her. It was really quite simple: Tia's reassignment would likely make it harder for Jannie to complete her own work. Keeping that in mind, she tried to see things from her supervisor's perspective. Later, Jannie met with her supervisor privately. She began, "Clearly, I'm troubled by Tia's reassignment. I handled this poorly in the meeting and I'd like to try again." The supervisor encouraged her to go on. "Being successful at my job is really important. I'm concerned that Tia's work on this other project means she won't be contributing as much to the team's effort. I know it's important to make our quarterly goals, so would you be willing to discuss some ideas for how we can make our quarterly goals while allowing Tia to work on the other project? Maybe together we can come up with a plan." Jannie's supervisor agreed and after talking through several options, they decided to bring in an intern to complete the routine tasks of Tia's job. The solution relieved Jannie's concerns about making her quarterly goals, and it also improved things for Tia, who now felt confident she could work on the new project without harming the team.

Using our voice to integrate our concerns with the interests of others has three benefits. First, it reminds us that other people have concerns that are as important to them as ours are to us, and this is easy to forget when we're feeling troubled. Second, it shows we are not just complaining about the trouble; rather, we are focusing on positive solutions. Third, it invites people to join with us. When they see how they will benefit and that real dialogue is possible, they are far more likely to respond positively. This gives us a chance to work out troubles without sacrificing relationships.

Voicing your concerns is a high-commitment and active way to respond to troubles. The other high-commitment option is passive; loyalty means waiting for the troubles to pass while remaining positive.

Loyalty

The author of *The Gift of Fear*, Gavin de Becker, says he has a friend who has two drawers in his desk at work: one for things he must do something about, and one for things that will pass on their own with time. When you suspect the trouble will resolve on its own, or more communication won't improve it, two practices can greatly assist you in remaining loyal to your commitment despite troubles. You can *accept ongoing challenges* and *maintain positive illusions*.

Accepting ongoing challenges. Any commitment will have ongoing challenges. All activities, jobs, and relationships will present hurdles that cannot simply be eliminated. The key is to develop a mind-set that allows you to accept the difficulties and minimize their impact. When you learn to look past challenges and focus on what you treasure, ongoing challenges don't have to overwhelm you.

This principle is clearly demonstrated in committed relationships. Have you ever found yourself having the same argument with a loved one again and again? If so, you're far from alone. According to Gottman and his decades of research, 69 percent of marital issues are what he calls *perpetual problems*. Perpetual problems reflect fundamental differences between people in which there is no "solution" that will permanently resolve the conflict. Perhaps a couple has fundamentally different visions about how to keep a clean house, raise kids, or vote. Such challenges don't have neat solutions that allow us to agree, move on, and never revisit the topic again. Instead, married couples will find these ongoing issues hanging around for the next five, ten, or fifty years.

Now, before panic sets in over the knowledge that the foremost expert on marriage and divorce found that more than two-thirds of marital problems don't have a solution, understand that in stable marriages husbands and wives are not overly troubled by their differences. They accept ongoing challenges as part of the relationship and may even see the humor in them. These couples understand that difficulties will always be there. They acknowledge the issue is there, but try not to let it bother them too much. In unstable marriages, perpetual problems lead to gridlock. Differences send partners further and further apart. Husband and wives have the same conversation again and again, with the same heat behind it. As time goes on, they become more certain of their own convictions and more convinced the other is wrong. They feel increasingly hurt and rejected by their differences.

It's helpful to realize there are ongoing issues in any relationship, even the happiest ones. If you move on to a different commitment, it means you're moving on to a different set of challenges. Of course, some differences are more troubling than others. The important question when it comes to commitment is: Are the challenges in this relationship ones you can cope with and learn to accept? Let's say that your partner, Mr. X, is often late and you feel hurt and disrespected. You regularly try to convince him that it is important to be on time. Meanwhile, Mr. X feels terribly controlled whenever you try to tell him "where to be and when." If you had made another choice and picked Mr. Y, you wouldn't have this problem. Mr. Y would be home at two in the afternoon from his going-nowhere part-time job, watching *Law and Order* reruns. You wouldn't argue with him about respect and time; instead you'd have a repetitive conflict over what it means to have "life goals." Whomever you're with, there will be challenging differences. The question is, which set of circumstances can you come to take lightly? In satisfying and lasting relationships, you'll partner with someone whose differences don't devastate you. Instead of fighting against those differences, you'll show your loyalty by managing them as good-naturedly as possible.

An additional way to remain loyal despite troubles is to see your situation through rose-colored glasses.

Maintaining positive illusions. Every week, Garrison Keillor hosts a radio program from the fictional town of Lake Wobegon, where "all the women are strong, all the men are good-looking, and all the children are above average." His program is intended to be humorous, but Keillor is onto an important finding in social science research. While not everyone can be above average, most of us rate ourselves above the norm on everything from looks to intelligence. We have what psychology researchers call *positive illusions*, or an unrealistically optimistic view of ourselves. Although this is considered a bias in perception, seeing ourselves in the best light is essential to our happiness, well-being, and ability to persist in the face of setbacks.

Positive illusions are useful in committed relationships. Rusbult and her colleagues from the University of North Carolina asked dating and married couples to fill out questionnaires. Some couples reported on perceptions of their own relationships, whereas others reported on perceptions of their "closest friend's" relationships or the "average" relationship. Participants rated things like the relationship's quality and their optimism about the future of the relationship. The results showed that people tend to believe their own relationship is better than others' relationships, and this positive illusion is associated with higher levels of commitment. The more committed we are, the better we think our relationship is relative to others'.

With high commitment, not only do you have an idealized view of your relationship; you also have an idealized view of your partner. When she is overly cranky, you blame her workload. When he is overly picky, you remind yourself he has high standards. You have to—if you made negative interpretations you wouldn't want to stay. Positive illusions allow you to maximize your partner's virtues and minimize his or her faults. Researchers from the University of Waterloo, in Ontario, Canada, had nearly two hundred couples complete questionnaires regarding their perception of themselves and their partners on a variety of positive qualities, like being kind and self-assured, and on a variety of faults, like being thoughtless and controlling. For the most part, people saw their partners in the same way the partners saw themselves. But there was one exception: In highly satisfying relationships, people saw their partners even better than the partners saw themselves.

When your goal is to maintain commitment in spite of a trouble you may not be able to fix, one of the ways you can respond is with loyalty—the practice of thinking positively despite the difficult moments. You can embrace loyalty by accepting ongoing challenges and maintaining positive illusions.

Voice and loyalty are appropriate when your goal is to increase commitment in a relationship or in the workplace. If you are interested in increasing commitment to a personal or professional goal, however, you have to get gritty.

True Grit

The four strategies described previously—neglect, exit, voice, and loyalty—can be appropriately used to respond to dissatisfaction in the workplace and in relationships. Grit is a behavior or personal trait that is particularly powerful when your commitment involves a long-term goal, like getting a degree, starting a company, or mastering a sport. In social science research, the term *grit* is relatively new, but the concept has been around a long time. Over the years, scholars have noticed that IQ doesn't seem to predict high or low levels of achievement as much as perseverance, practice, and long-term effort do. *Grit* is the proclivity to persevere in the face of challenges. It means continuing to bring your best effort despite adversity. It allows you to sustain involvement and interest over the long haul, despite troubles along the way.

The leading researcher in this area is Angela Duckworth, a psychology professor at the University of Pennsylvania. Duckworth and her coauthors first became interested in the idea of grit when they noticed a trend in their interview data. They had been interviewing people in a variety of careers about what makes a "star performer." As much as interviewees mentioned talent, they talked about a quality that sounded a lot like grit. They respected and admired their peers who seemed to make up for lack of innate talent by maintaining a commitment to their goals despite setbacks. Similarly, they pointed out there are naturally gifted people who don't make it to the top of their fields because they lack this quality.

Since there wasn't a tool in the research to measure a person's level of grit, Duckworth and her colleagues decided to build one. They developed a questionnaire for measuring two qualities of grit: *sustained effort* and *consistency of interests*. Sustained effort refers to overcoming setbacks to conquer important challenges, and achieving goals that take years of work. Consistency of interests refers to sticking with a goal rather than choosing a different one later, and holding the same interests year after year.

Above-average grit scores have been shown to predict higher education levels, fewer career changes, and higher grade point averages. While grit is associated with higher GPAs, it is not related to higher SAT scores. SAT is the standardized test that measures a student's general skill in writing, critical reading, and math. It appears that while gritty students enter college with average SAT scores, they nonetheless earn higher GPAs than their peers, through determination and sustained effort.

A case in point was a study of grit among spelling bee competitors. Participants in the Scripps National Spelling Bee filled out scales that measured verbal IQ and grit. They also indicated how many hours per week they had studied for the competition. Next, researchers tracked how far the competitors advanced before they were eliminated. Those with above-average grit scores were 40 percent more likely to advance to further rounds than their same-age peers. Verbal IQ also predicted further advancement, even though verbal IQ and grit were not associated with each other. How can it be that there's no relationship between verbal IQ and grit, even though both predicted advancement in the bee? It turns out, our gritty spelling bee participants had studied longer. They were able to make up for any reduced natural verbal ability with their determination. The researchers concluded, "Gritty children work longer and harder than their less gritty peers and, as a consequence, perform better."

If you have an important or challenging goal, don't underestimate the power of grit. If you aren't lucky, brilliant, or naturally gifted, you will have to expend more effort and be willing to persevere through challenges. But here's the good news: Grit works. And it appears it works as well as or better than having innate gifts, like a high IQ. So if you really want something, no excuses. Stick with it, and celebrate what your perseverance is able to accomplish.

Moving Forward

Troubles play a powerful role in your level of satisfaction and commitment, and as it turns out, you need quite a few treasures to make up for the inevitable troubles you'll encounter in relationships, jobs, and fulfilling long-term goals. Some troubles are a relatively small price to pay for a commitment that brings a lot of meaning to your life. Others are created by your negative interpretation of events—and that's good news, because as you consider other "stories," your experience of those troubles can decrease. However, some troubles are very real, and these require a response.

People respond to troubles with a variety of strategies. In some cases, you'll realize the troubles associated with working for this company are too substantial relative to what you gain, and thus you'll begin to look for other choices and ultimately leave. In other circumstances, you'll speak up and actively work to solve the problem. You can use your voice constructively and discover solutions that improve the situation for everyone. Sometimes you'll remain loyal to a relationship through internal choices like accepting perpetual problems and seeing the best in your partner. Finally, when it comes to a long-term goal, you might get gritty and vow not to let troubles stop you. Your decision will be based on the magnitude of the treasures relative to troubles, and will also depend on the impact of the next two elements of the Commitment Equation, contributions and choices.

The Takeaway
Using Knowledge of Troubles to Affect Your Commitment Goals

All In

If you are interested in going all in, you'll benefit from investigating how the troubling aspects of the situation can be managed, minimized, or accepted. Consider one or more of the following avenues for doing so.

- Because the negative will likely impact you more than the positive, consciously remind yourself of the things you treasure when troubles emerge.

- Because it takes about five positives to balance out a negative, take any opportunity you can to create positive interactions.

- When a troubling event occurs, notice the story you tell yourself. Instead of sticking with the story, go back to the facts and see what other stories could be told.

- In the face of troubles, it may be tempting to exit emotionally or physically. Instead, speak up. Use your voice in a way that takes others' needs into account as well as your own.

- In the face of troubles, it may be tempting to neglect the commitment and let it slowly deteriorate. Instead, remain loyal by accepting there are perpetual problems in any commitment and choosing to see the situation in the best possible light.

- When all else fails, get gritty. Decide you will persevere no matter what challenges are put in your way.

Moving On

If you are interested in moving on, it's time to take a realistic look at your troubles. Consider one or more of the following avenues for starting the process to de-commit.

- Consider whether the negatives have come to consistently outweigh the positives.

- Consider whether the existing troubles are changeable. If they are not, be honest about whether you can accept them.

- If you have already tried to make the best interpretation of the troubling situation, be honest about whether or not the facts themselves are unacceptable.

- Be honest about whether your previous attempts at voice and loyalty have made any improvements.

- Consider giving yourself some space from the commitment to see how you feel. Giving yourself some time away will help you discover whether there is a way to commit in a different way.

- Consider whether this activity still reflects who you are and what you want.

Assisting Others

If you are interested in assisting others to higher commitment, identify ways to manage or minimize the troubles they experience. Consider one or more of the following avenues for doing so.

- Be aware that the negative impacts people more than the positive at a rate of five to one. Provide as many positive experiences as you can to balance out the inevitable negatives.

- Alternatively, discover the one thing that is particularly troubling to others and remove it. Because troubles are powerful, removing even one negative can have a significant impact on levels of satisfaction.

- When someone comes to you with a troubling story about your behavior, compassionately ask him to describe the facts that led him to that conclusion. Respectfully ask if the two of you can come up with a different story about those facts.

- Voice is associated with high levels of satisfaction and investment. When others use their voice to say that they are troubled by something, this is a good sign. Help them speak up without fear.

CHAPTER 5

Contributions: How Much Have You Given?

(Treasures – Troubles) + Contributions – Choices = Level of Commitment

IMAGINE a team in which every member brings his full participation every day. And imagine that while some members have a more glamorous position than others, everyone is equally respected for their contribution. Imagine they have a leader who won't take less than each member's personal best. And imagine that as a result of being on this team, the members see themselves as having a greater source of strength and resilience than they knew.

Or, instead of imagining, you could watch Chris Petersen run his college football program. Petersen, as mentioned in Chapter 3, is a Paul "Bear" Bryant Award–winning coach who has led his previously not-so-well-known team to big wins every year for the past seven years. This is due to a system he has developed for picking the right guys and getting them to contribute at the highest level. It begins during recruitment. Petersen looks for what every coach looks for—strength, good hands, speed; the usual performance traits. But he also looks for something else: whether the guy loves football—I mean really treasures the sport. Petersen says that on a scale of 1 to 10, his players need to treasure football at level 12, because it takes that kind of love of the game to succeed in a program in which troubles like long hours, grueling physical endurance, and constant surveillance are the norm. To be successful, players can't just give it their all on game day. They must go all in every day and in most aspects of their lives: on the practice field, in the weight room, in the classroom, on campus, and in the community. And they have to be willing to make sacrifices. They may not get the position they want or get to play in a game right away. They are expected to attend classes and maintain their lockers to code. They must forgo the typical college-party mayhem. Petersen's players give up a lot. From what I can tell, they give their whole lives for four years to this all-encompassing cause. On Petersen's team, contributions and commitment are one and the same. Because the players are committed, they contribute at a high level, and as they contribute, they become increasingly committed.

The Meaning of Contributions

Commitment is created in large part by the treasure-to-trouble evaluation that occurs in your mind, but it's also created by what you do. Each time you bring your creativity to a work project, spend money on a date, or give your all to the football team, you increase your level of commitment. These actions, which I call *contributions*, lead you to feel connected and take a higher level of ownership. Contributions increase your devotion to something rewarding, like being on a winning team, but they also increase your attachment to things that no longer get positive returns. In this way, contributions are neutral—they work to increase your commitment whether the outcome of that commitment is beneficial or not.

Contributions consist of resources you invest in a project or a relationship that you can't fully recover if you quit or leave. These resources vary from the tangible, like financial investments, to the intangible, like giving your time and effort. Of the four elements of the Commitment Equation, you have the most control over contributions. You decide where to invest yourself. You decide how to spend your money and where to give your creative effort. And the decision you make about where and how you will contribute matters.

Where Resources Go, Commitment Will Grow

Contributions fall into four broad categories, which I call *time*, *talent*, *tenderness*, and *tangibles*.

- *Time* refers to the minutes, hours, days, or years you give to something or someone. It also includes the effort that goes into those hours or days. It might include, for example, the years you've spent at your job.
- *Talent* refers to your contribution of skill, ideas, and creativity. It might include the skills you had that allowed you to remodel your home.
- *Tenderness* refers to contributions of the heart, like caring for another person's well-being or trusting him or her with personal information about yourself.
- *Tangibles* consist of money and the concrete resources

money can buy. It might include getting a loan to go back to school.

The various forms of contribution often co-occur. My hairstylist, Kim, has dated several men since her divorce eight years ago, but something seems different in her current relationship. She says that thanks to her man, she's now able to park in the garage for the first time since buying her home. The two-car garage had been used primarily as storage until her boyfriend reorganized it so she could drive her car into one side of the space. She was thrilled to finally use the garage for its intended purpose, until she thought about her dogs. They too used the garage, for naps and food, and she didn't want them going on a field trip whenever she opened the garage door. So her boyfriend went to Home Depot and developed a configuration that allowed the dogs to get their food without the risk of doggie dine-and-dash. I remarked to Kim that she was dating a talented man. If you think about it, though, he contributed more than his talent. He also contributed his time and several tangibles, including money for supplies and tools to build the kennel. He even contributed tenderness, as he thought about her needs. According to a large body of evidence, contributions like these not only reflect her boyfriend's current level of commitment; they also serve to *increase* his commitment (and probably Kim's as well, since she treasures his contributions). Soon after overhauling the garage, he agreed to spend the week of Christmas at the home of Kim's parents, who live out of state; another sign of increased commitment.

Here's what we know about how contributions affect commitment. There are three primary mechanisms, which I've gleaned from a variety of fields like psychology, business, and economics.

I'll refer to them as the *Accumulation Effect*, the *Value Effect*, and the *Entrapment Effect*.

1. *The Accumulation Effect*—When small, seemingly inconsequential contributions add up to a more significant contribution.
2. *The Value Effect*—When contributions lead us to value a relationship or project.
3. *The Entrapment Effect*—When contributions lead us to stay with a commitment, even when it's costly or not in our best interest.

We often think commitment precedes contribution, that if a person is committed to a cause then she'll contribute to it. In reality, contribution often precedes commitment. Our actions drive our level of commitment as much as our level of commitment drives our actions. If a person contributes to a cause, *then* she'll likely be committed to it. Let's take a look at how this works.

The Accumulation Effect

You may not think much of the little contributions you make each day, but they encourage your future behavior. As psychologist Robert Cialdini has said, small initial commitments have a tendency to "grow their own legs." Let's say you're walking around your local farmer's market, where producers are selling their organic tomatoes and handmade pottery. Some booths are for local causes. As you walk by this section, a kindly woman pops out from a booth and asks if you would sign a petition to establish a social club for people with disabilities. This seems like a reasonable request. You care about people and she's only asking for a signature, so you say yes. You sign the petition and as you turn to walk away, she asks if you would be willing to make a donation to this important cause. If you're like most people, you are more likely to agree to the larger request of donating to the cause after agreeing to the smaller request of signing the petition. Psychologist Joseph Schwarzwald and his colleagues discovered that people who were first invited to sign the petition were more likely to contribute—and to contribute larger amounts—than those who were asked for a donation without first being asked to sign the petition.

Many marketers are aware of this effect. They know that if they can get you to make a small effort, you are more likely to become loyal to their product. You may have noticed that many competition TV shows contain a "voting" element. On *American Idol*, for example, the audience is invited to place their vote via the Internet. They can also have their choice reflected on their Facebook page. On *Top Chef*, viewers are encouraged to text their opinion on any number of issues, such as "Who is *your* Top Chef?" and "Is Lorena a help or a hindrance in the kitchen?" Television shows don't set up these kinds of interactive contributions for fun. They do it because the acts of calling in, tweeting, texting, and clicking are small contributions that connect you to the show and increase the likelihood of larger contributions, like tuning in week after week.

While much of the research on this effect occurs in the context of donations and marketing, there are many areas of our lives where it applies. All of us at some time have experienced a commitment that simply "grew legs." I recall that whenever I auditioned for a play, invariably I wanted the role far more after the audition than I did before. Sometimes I think I only wanted the part because of the effort I put into the audition, and not because the part was inherently valuable to me. Watch any reality show and you'll see the participants become more determined to stay in the competition the further along they get. And when they finally do get voted off, many look into the camera and say, "I'm more committed than ever to developing my craft and showing the world what I have to offer." I have yet to hear someone say, "After that experience, my interest in singing [or cooking or dancing] has certainly diminished." As their contributions steadily accumulate, their commitment grows as well.

If you want others to commit, begin by asking for small contributions. I met with a student who was attempting to put together a committee for his thesis. Knowing many professors feel overworked and over-obligated, I suggested, as a first step, that he simply meet with faculty members, share his research idea, and ask for their advice. Don't ask them to be on your committee right out of the gates, I said. Their first reaction might be to say no because they have too many other obligations. First, get them to contribute their ideas, because then they'll have a small stake in what you are doing. Later, when you ask them to be on your committee, they will be more inclined to say yes since they've had a hand in developing your thesis idea.

Since contributions accumulate, you have an opportunity to reflect on where you contribute even small amounts of your time, talent, tenderness, and tangibles. You might think these are minor decisions, but they can gain momentum. And this is a wonderful thing. When you are in the right relationship, your contributions of doing the laundry or sharing personal information are bonding you with your loved one. When you are in the right organization, it's great that each time you bring coffee cake or help solve a problem your connection to the organization grows stronger. On the other hand, this wonderful ability of commitment to accumulate and grow legs can also bond you to a project that's wrong for you, and you can end up feeling stuck. You may one day look around and wonder, "How did I get here?" But the good news is this. When you are aware of how contributions accumulate and build commitment, you can more mindfully contribute to the areas of your life you find most meaningful, and pull back on the areas that are harmful or no longer important to you.

Let's say you're committed to something that isn't right for you—a person or a project—but because of the contributions you've made, you're having a tough time letting go. It's difficult to *will* yourself to walk away. If you're attached, you're attached, even if it's to something that no longer serves you. A better strategy is to proactively reduce your contributions. When I decided to write this book, I needed to regroup and re-prioritize various aspects of my life. I reluctantly decided to stop playing tennis for a couple of years to focus on the research and writing that was ahead of me. The problem was I was hopelessly committed to tennis. After seven years of competitive play, my contributions had nearly accumulated to the point of no return. I had invested a lot of money in equipment and lessons, I belonged to a club and a team, I had a steady practice partner, and I was on many tennis-related e-mail lists. Initially, I didn't know how to make the feeling of attachment go away, even though I recognized the need to do so. After agonizing about it for some time, I decided to take steps to reduce my contributions: I asked to be taken off the round-robin list at my club, I asked to be removed from the event e-mail lists, and I explained to my practice partner I wouldn't be available. Through these actions, I naturally started to feel less committed. I stopped thinking about what I was missing and focused instead on the new opportunity in front of me. While Cialdini never mentioned it in his writings, reducing your contributions can grow legs too, and it can assist you when you need to let go.

You are in charge of what you do with your time, talent, tenderness, and tangibles. Whatever you contribute to, even in small amounts, will gain energy and importance. What you don't contribute to will lose energy and importance. Where resources go, commitment will grow, and you get to decide where that is.

The Value Effect

Imagine you are standing in the middle of an IKEA store. Everything from coffee tables to media furniture is in that Scandinavian modern style, at reasonable prices. And that's the reason for IKEA's success, isn't it—the Scandinavian modern style, at reasonable prices? It turns out there's more to the story, and something more basic may contribute to IKEA's continued success: They make you build your own stuff.

Perhaps you've noticed that when you contribute to something you tend to value it more. A team of researchers from Harvard, Princeton, and Duke wanted to find out if this was a real and predictable effect, so they invited people into the lab and put them in one of two groups: the build-it group or the inspect-it group. The build-it group received the materials and instructions necessary to build an IKEA product—in this case, a black storage box. The inspect-it group didn't build a box, but was given an identical premade box to examine. The researchers asked participants, whether builders or inspectors, to consider two questions: How much do you like this box? How much do you think this box is worth?

Imagine for a moment that you're in this study and you have a black storage box sitting in front of you. If you're in the inspect-it group, this box came out of nowhere. You had nothing to do with its creation. It's a plain old box, probably one of dozens of similar products, so it has no personal meaning to you. But if you're in the build-it group, you put your sweat equity into this thing. You put in your time and effort and some vision, and because of this, maybe you see more than a product. Maybe you see more than constructed materials, but a part of yourself, and the pride that comes from creation. Indeed, the researchers found that the two groups valued their boxes differently. The people in the build-it group were fond of the result. They had far higher appreciation than those who inspected a premade box. And when they estimated the box's value, the build-it group indicated an average dollar amount 63 percent higher than the price determined by the inspectors of an identical box. Clearly, the build-it people and the inspect-it people saw the product differently.

While the researchers called this the *IKEA Effect*, they found this phenomenon occurred with other products as well. They replicated the process with origami, those colorful paper sheets you fold into birds and other animal shapes. Some participants followed the instructions to make their own small crane or frog, and others inspected identical premade cranes and frogs. Once again, those who made their own origami saw the end result differently, and valued their creations 460 percent higher than inspectors valued their premade objects. We value not only outcomes; we value our contribution to those outcomes. Our effort, our time, and our creativity make a difference. The more we engage in a process, the more we value the result.

Here is a simple exercise that will help you relate to the IKEA Effect. Go to your kitchen and retrieve a chef's knife from its stored location. Now, analyze its quality and decide the value, in dollars, you place on the knife. Now pretend instead that you had to make the knife. Imagine you had to locate and obtain the materials the knife would be made from and that you had to create the classic design that suits chefs and home cooks so well. Think about how important this knife is to the end user in terms of preparing meals for family or customers, and think about its contribution to the culinary world. Now how much do you value the knife? This is obviously a rudimentary exercise, but it gets at the heart of the power of our contributions. We value things more when we have a hand in their creation.

Using Contributions to Increase Value and Commitment

Sixteen faculty members, including me, were in a department meeting discussing potential changes to the course listings for our graduate program. The changes recommended by a three-person graduate committee were substantial, and many people in the room were not in support. In fact, the discussion was filled with annoyance and skepticism about whether the proposal would work. If the committee were to try to force the proposal on the group, they would be met with resistance or, in the best-case scenario, unenthusiastic compliance. The meeting was at a standstill.

Then, one of the faculty members stood up and went to the whiteboard. She wasn't on the committee or a designated leader, but she offered this idea: "How about if we list all the classes on the board that we would need to teach with this proposal, and find out who among us is excited about each one? If a class gets no support, we delete it. Those with support, we keep." This seemed an acceptable process, and at least a way to move forward, so each class was listed. One class at a time, the volunteer leader asked, "What about this course? Does anyone feel passionate about it? Is anyone willing to claim it?" For the first class, three professors said it was important and they would teach it. She wrote their names next to the class. For the subsequent class, two professors said it was important and they'd take ownership for it. Three members claimed the next course, and so on. As the faculty talked about what was important to them and took ownership for certain courses, the energy in the room began to change. By the end of the hour, all eighteen courses were spoken for, and each person seemed dedicated to his or her part of the job. A vote was called, and the proposal unanimously passed.

How could a group of strong-willed, disagreeable professors go from shaking heads and folded arms to smiles and relaxed shoulders in the space of an hour? How could a proposal go from being viewed with suspicion and distance to being viewed with enthusiasm and connection? *The difference was the opportunity to contribute.* As faculty members invested themselves in the proposed courses, they began to take ownership, and that made the difference.

Contributions tend to increase the value we attach to the things in our lives. When we contribute to building something, for example, we instinctively feel a greater sense of pride and ownership in the outcome. But just because contributions are a powerful tool to enhance commitment doesn't mean they always lead us to commit to the right things. Contributions in themselves are neutral. They don't know whether this is the right relationship or the right career for you. But when you invest your time, talent, tenderness, and tangibles your attachment will be increased whether it's a good fit or not.

The Entrapment Effect

When you make contributions, you are more likely to stay with a project even when it becomes clear that the course you're on is costly. This is called *entrapment*, and you've probably experienced it to a mild extent waiting for a slow elevator. The elevator is taking a while, so it occurs to you to take the stairs. The longer you stand there, the more you want to take the stairs, but the more compelled you feel to stick it out given the time you've already put into waiting. Jeffrey Rubin and Joel Brockner, psychologists from Tufts University, wanted to discover what factors increase our feelings of entrapment.

Imagine you're a college student and you agree to be part of Rubin and Brockner's experiment. You're told it's a study about how groups solve problems when resources are scarce. You're ushered into a private cubicle, where you see a stopwatch, a set of instructions, and your "initial stake" of $2.40. By the way, it's 1975. You're wearing bell-bottoms, and that $2.40 would buy a movie ticket and a six-pack of beer. You read the instructions and learn you're part of a four-person group. Each person in your group will engage in the same task, individually: solving a crossword puzzle. The puzzle has ten words, and if you can solve eight of the ten words within three minutes, you'll win the jackpot—eight dollars. But if you take more than three minutes or solve fewer than eight words, your earnings are systematically reduced as described in the instructions. For example, if you get all eight words, but it takes you four minutes instead of three, you get the jackpot minus 10 percent. You also learn that some of the words will be challenging, and for those you can rely on a crossword dictionary.

But there's a catch. They tell you that since this is a study about "problem solving under conditions of scarce resources," there is only one dictionary for all four people in your group to share, so if someone else is using it, you'll have to wait in line. In addition, you can't wait in line and work on the puzzle at the same time. If and when you want the dictionary, you have to flip a switch on the wall of your cubicle, and if no one else is using it, the experimenter will bring it right over. But if the dictionary is in use, the experimenter will bring a card indicating your place in line, whether first, second, or third, and your puzzle will be temporarily removed. You can ask for the puzzle back at anytime and continue working, but you'll lose your place in line. You can also stop solving the puzzle at any time and receive whatever funds you're due with the amount of time spent and the number of words solved.

And so you begin. You get a few of the words, but the experimenter was right, some of these words are hard. You're going to need that dictionary. One minute has passed, so you better try to get the dictionary now. You flip your switch, and the experimenter takes your puzzle away and gives you a card indicating that you are first in line for the dictionary. Okay, that's good. Surely the other guy won't be using it for too long, given the time constraint. So you wait, and another minute goes by. You think about your puzzle. Three words are completed. There are four words for which you definitely need the dictionary. You may be able to get the remaining words on your own. You wait another ten seconds and your anxiety grows. Where is that dictionary? Should you ask for the puzzle back? You've already been waiting for the dictionary for what, one and a half minutes? Surely things will turn around any moment now. Crap, the three-minute mark just passed. Now you have no chance at the jackpot. You can't take it anymore. You give in at three and a half minutes and realize that with the few words you solved, you're owed about $1.80. Oh well, at least that still buys the beer.

This description reflects what the majority of the participants in this study experienced. They flipped their switch, got a card indicating their place in the "line," had their puzzle taken away, and never received a dictionary. Meanwhile, as they waited, their payout decreased by the minute. The dirty little secret that made this possible? There was no dictionary. There were no other players. The experimenters set the whole thing up to study one thing: the experience of psychological entrapment. In a situation more intense than waiting for an elevator, these students surely experienced the internal conflict of wanting to pull out, but also wanting to remain to make good on the time they'd already invested. Most often, it was the latter that won. More than half of the participants continued waiting for the dictionary beyond the point that they would have broken even. As a group, they spent about a third of their time waiting for a dictionary that would never arrive and received equal to or less than their initial stake. (Perhaps you see why this effect is sometimes called the *gambler's fallacy*.)

Some players became more entrapped than others, based on a few factors controlled by the researchers. The first was whether the participants' losses were "salient," that is, whether their losses were made obvious. All participants saw the loss schedule in the directions, but some participants also got to see a visual depiction of their moment-by-moment losses on a chart. People who could see the chart spent significantly less time waiting for the dictionary—they quit the puzzle earlier and earned more money. In daily life it isn't always easy to detect when something is steadily declining. For example, when does it become clear that your "cost effective" house remodel is becoming a financial burden? If the pattern of loss isn't obvious—if the contractor isn't regularly telling you how much you're over budget—your losses aren't salient and you may persevere beyond the point at which it would be best to change course.

The second factor was how far off the participants believed the goal was. Some were informed they were third in line for the dictionary, while some were told they were first in line. Those who thought they were further away from the goal, that is, third in line for the dictionary, ended up doing better. They spent less time waiting and earned more money. Meanwhile, the people who thought they were *almost there* became more determined to stick it out, even to their detriment. Thinking that you're making progress, that you're almost there, can sometimes be a hazard. If you think the remodel is almost done, while in fact it may be months away, you're more likely to stick to an unwise plan.

The third factor that influenced entrapment was how fast the funds got sucked away. Some participants were given a "rapid loss schedule," while others lost money more slowly. Those who lost money rapidly ended up with more cash in the end. When funds declined slowly, the losses were more difficult to notice, so participants held on past the point of good returns. A similar pattern can be seen among stock investors. If a stock declines slowly, the owner may not recognize her losses until they are significant. But at that point, she's entrapped: Part of her wants to sell the stock before she loses even more, but part of her wants to stay with the stock because selling it now would mean turning a possibly temporary loss into a definitely permanent one. If her loss had been rapid, she might have been jolted into selling while she was still ahead. In sum, it appears we are most at risk for entrapment when we aren't paying close attention to our costs or losses, when we're convinced we're getting close to a positive outcome, and when losses come slowly.

When you're working toward a goal, like developing a product, you make contributions toward that goal. As we've discussed, the more you contribute, the more committed you are likely to become. Sometimes you'll find that you have contributed far more than you expected at the onset, and the goal has not been reached. You may experience an internal conflict—part of you wants to persevere in hopes that you can still achieve the goal, and part of you wants to cut your losses and let go before you've contributed any more. This is an important decision point. It's helpful to pause and take an honest look at where you are. Are you getting closer to your goal, and do you feel good about your progress? If you invest more, will it lead to the meaningful outcome you want? Or are you in a situation in which you are investing far more of your resources than makes sense given the value of the project?

In a surprising number of cases, we keep going even though we are no longer getting beneficial returns. Sometimes we stay with something *only* because of previous investments and not because we are getting a positive outcome. This is the phenomenon economists have termed the *sunk cost fallacy* and Allan Teger, psychologist turned visual artist, calls *too-much-invested-to-quit*.

Too-Much-Invested-to-Quit

The other night my husband and I were watching *The Voice* and two singers were competing to stay on the show. Their fate was up to a coach/judge who had worked with one of the contestants for a longer period of time than the other. His newer singer seemed far more talented (at least according to us, all three of the other judges, and the viewers who commented on NBC.com), but the coach/judge picked the inferior singer, saying, "I have so much time invested in Julio, I've got to go with Julio." Here the judge was aware that his commitment to Julio was unduly influenced by sunk costs, and yet he made the decision anyway.

Why do previous contributions make it so hard to let go of undesirable commitments? Why don't we do what's right for us now, rather than basing our decision on the time and effort we've given in the past? One explanation from psychological theory is that we don't like to be wasteful. When we put in our time or money, we think we should stay with it even if that means sticking with something that isn't working or that no longer appeals to us. It's like listening to a terrible band because you already paid the $20 cover charge. The truth is this: You've lost the $20 either way. It's gone. At this point, you can either a) lose $20 and have a lousy time at the concert, or b) lose $20 and leave to enjoy your evening doing something else.

On the other hand, being too-much-invested-to-quit in the important areas of your life can be a great thing. Deeply investing in a meaningful long-term relationship is a great use of your contributions. Even the most important relationships in our lives won't feel positive every day. Without contributions, we might just quit whenever the troubling part of the relationship temporarily outweighs the part we treasure. How wonderful that we have the glue of contribution to help us stick with our commitments, even on tough days. Remember, though, that contributions in themselves are neutral: They are constructive when they bind us to a meaningful project, and detrimental when they bind us to a project that's harmful.

Research on entrepreneurs provides an example of how contributions can bind us to a project whether that's a good decision or not. Business and economics researchers tell us that if we were purely logical, our decision to stay with an entrepreneurial venture would be based exclusively on market feedback. Favorable feedback should lead us to expand and be more committed, and negative feedback should lead us to contract and reduce our commitment. But a logical assessment of the market isn't the only thing that influences our decisions.

Anne McCarthy and a research team from the Department of Management at Indiana University tracked more than a thousand new entrepreneurial firms to discover what psychological factors increased the likelihood a new business would still be operating a year after it opened. A key factor was whether the entrepreneur had started the business himself or whether he'd bought or inherited an existing venture. Both starting a business and buying a business require contributions, but think about how much more investment goes into starting a business from scratch. Capital is certainly involved, and so are creativity, personal energy, long hours, and likely a lot of heart. Not surprising given what we know about contributions, those who'd started a business were more likely than those who'd purchased a business to increase investments in the company a year later. This is a powerful testament to how increased contributions can create greater commitment to important areas of our lives. But McCarthy's work also reflected a potential downside: These entrepreneurs were even more likely to invest additional resources one year later when the market feedback was *negative* rather than positive.

At first glance, this seems counterintuitive. Why would entrepreneurs contribute *more* to something that's failing? Why wouldn't they recognize the negative market feedback as a signal to change course? One reason is that after all the time, talent, tenderness, and tangibles they have invested, they're attached to seeing the business succeed. All of the previous contributions, which they don't want to admit were a mistake, can lead them to overlook important indicators that the business is failing and thus doesn't deserve more time and resources. Another reason for their persistence, according to McCarthy's research, is overconfidence in their ability to make it work. Being overconfident may have helped them get started, as it gave them the passion, excitement, energy, and vision needed to do their best. But later that very trait may lead them to make unwise decisions, like continuing to invest in a business that's on a failing course.

It is often difficult to tell whether something has a chance of turning around. When you know about the entrapment effect, one of the things you can do is set comfortable limits for yourself. You can decide, "I'll give it everything I have for the next six months, and if I don't have a minimum of seventy-five customers, I'll move on to another option." Then if you find you're continuing to break the limits you set, you'll recognize you're being negatively influenced by the too-much-invested-to-quit effect. Another option is to seek independent feedback from someone who isn't invested in your business and can give an objective opinion. It's hard to accept that not every venture or relationship will succeed, but the victory is assessing the situation honestly and making a positive long-term choice based on that assessment. As stated by F. Scott Fitzgerald, "Vitality shows not only in the ability to persist, but in the ability to start over."

The normal, human tendency to feel too-much-invested-to-quit isn't necessarily bad (it's great if the commitment ultimately works out), but we need to be aware of this tendency in order to reduce the chances it will unconsciously drive decisions that aren't in our best interest. We have the opportunity to pay attention at critical moments when we are going to either increase contributions or back off. Ideally, we will make this decision consciously, based on our deepest values. And we will make the decision based on realistic feedback, rather than being overly influenced by past investments.

Sliding Versus Deciding

The ability to maintain a high level of commitment is a large part of what makes us wonderful spouses or successful business owners. On the other hand, there are people and projects we stay with, even though we never consciously decided to do so. Perhaps we made small contributions that led to larger contributions, and even though something felt wrong along the way, we found ourselves with too-much-invested-to-quit.

A team of researchers from University of Denver's Center for Marital and Family Studies called this phenomenon *sliding versus deciding*. They came up with this concept when attempting to understand why couples who cohabitate before marriage have an increased risk for a variety of marital problems, including divorce. What's that, you say? People who live together before getting married are *more* likely to get a divorce? Indeed, those are the statistics, and in addition, marriages that begin with premarital cohabitation also experience poorer quality of communication, increased negativity, lower satisfaction, reduced relationship quality, and more physical aggression. That's a concerning list the researchers didn't want to ignore. Particularly intriguing is that these problems do not occur to the same degree among premarital cohabitators who were engaged before moving in together. Even though they are also cohabitating before marriage, their marriage ends up looking more like the marriage of a couple who didn't cohabitate. So what's going on with these non-engaged premaritally cohabitating couples that puts them at an increased risk, and what can they tell us about contributions and commitment?

As discussed in Chapter 1, commitment can be understood as consisting of two general forces: dedication and constraint. Recall that dedication is the "want to" part of commitment. In the context of romantic love and marriage, it consists of our strong desire to share our life with this particular person. Constraint is the "have to" part of commitment. It's the part that makes us feel we must stay because the costs of leaving are too high. As we've seen in this chapter, contributions often strengthen the feeling we have to stay. When we've decided we're personally dedicated, adding constraints is a wonderful way to strengthen our commitment.

But what if we aren't sure about the relationship? Many cohabitators say they moved in with their partner because it was convenient or made sense financially. Many people, especially men, say they moved in together as a "test," to see if their relationship would work. Unfortunately, these reasons are not based on dedication. In fact, if we need to test the relationship, that may indicate an awareness of existing problems and concerns that this isn't the right match. So, while we haven't decided anything yet, here we are living with a person, which means significant investments. We may cosign a lease we can't afford individually, or adopt a pet together and open a joint bank account. We might paint and buy furnishings together. At the very least we put in far more time, energy, and effort than we would in a regular dating relationship. And we do all this without a clear, mutually agreed-upon plan for where we are headed.

Cohabitation increases the likelihood of marriage, but not necessarily because the test was "passed" and problems were resolved. It increases the likelihood of marriage because of the investments and constraints that make it harder to break up. We may marry someone whom we wouldn't have chosen to marry had we not been living together. The University of Denver team discovered that adding just *one* concrete investment, like buying furniture together, "increased the chances of staying together by 10% on average." Let me put it another way: Unmarried people may continue a relationship with a poorly matched partner because it's easier than deciding what to do with the co-owned Sony TV. Cohabitation itself is not the problem. Rather, it's the contributions that make it harder to leave. The experts call this *relationship inertia*.

Perhaps there is something we can learn from couples who planned to marry before moving in, given they're typically more successful down the road. Before packing up the U-Haul they had asked and answered the question "Who are we to each other and where are we headed?" They made a deliberate choice. They had a mutual understanding of what they wanted for their future, and *then* they made significant contributions to support their choice. Now, what if you are already living together? Are you doomed to slide, or can you still decide?

Justeen Long, a former student of mine, and her boyfriend, Scott, started out like many young cohabitating couples. She was living at her parents' house, so she and Scott spent all their time at his place. Even though they'd only known each other for a month, they seemed to love each other, so he invited her to officially move in. Justeen found his invitation amusing because she was nearly living there already, with her toothbrush on the sink and her PJs hanging on the bathroom door. But "officially" moving in meant she got to bring all of her things to the home, and she started contributing to the rent.

Although they were together constantly, they didn't talk about their relationship. By the time either one verbally said, "I love you," they'd been together a year. Before they knew it, three and a half years had gone by. They didn't think about marriage and didn't consider themselves people who wanted a "normal" life, but after that long together, the questions from family and friends started to come. "Why aren't you engaged?" "When are you getting married?" Many of their peers were getting married, so they finally decided to talk about it. According to Justeen, both she and Scott agreed they were afraid of marriage, which seemed ironic since they were clearly devoted to each other. Was it something about "solidifying the commitment" that scared them?

With questions unanswered, they bought a house together and moved in. They were like newlyweds, Justeen said, painting the walls, buying furniture, and getting the house organized just so. When two more years had passed, they looked at their lives and realized they weren't kids anymore. They'd met when Justeen was nineteen, but now they were both out of college, had jobs, and were active in their church and the community. They had to admit, marriage didn't sound so bad after all, and so they got engaged. Justeen didn't have a ring and no date was set, but the idea of marriage had become more real. As the magnitude of this commitment set in, she began to panic. She realized that because they'd met when they were so young, she'd never developed her own foundation or identity. She needed some time to clear her head and do some soul-searching. So she moved into her own apartment a mile down the road.

From a sliding-versus-deciding perspective, Justeen was giving herself the opportunity to make a clear and conscious decision, and she was allowing Scott the space to do the same. She had a chance to consider whether they were a good match, one to which she was personally dedicated, or whether she was only staying because of past contributions. During the time of her six-month lease, they lived apart but regularly came together to discuss their feelings. One of her primary concerns was that he was less devoted to their religion than she was, and she needed time to decide whether this was a difference she could live with. What she came to understand in their months apart is that all couples have differences. What matters is whether the differences are acceptable to each partner, and whether they have enough positives to create a healthy and happy bond. Together, Justeen and Scott finally decided to commit and make it work. By the time her lease was nearly up, Justeen felt clearer and she began moving her things back into their house. "Now we'll be stronger," she told me. "I had to make an actual decision about what matters, and that was really good learning for me."

Who knows what the future holds for Justeen and Scott, or for any of us? Commitment will continue to be a process. But Justeen has learned to make commitments in her life by choice and by design, rather than by default.

Moving Forward

Contributions are the resources you give to a career, a relationship, or a project. They include the money you invest, the time and creative effort you expend, and any occasion you give from the heart. Your contributions can generate positive results, like when the time and energy that went into a project increases your sense of ownership and gives you a deeper appreciation of the outcome. Contributions can also be potentially negative, like feeling entrapped because of sunk costs and feeling you "can't" stop what you're doing because you've already invested too much. Of the four elements that predict commitment, contributions is the one over which you have the most control. When you contribute less, your commitment will slow, and you can take time to consider your other choices. When you contribute more, your attachment and commitment will grow, and you'll be more likely to stick with it.

In the science of economics, business, and psychology, the terms associated with contributions tend to sound negative. Terms like *entrapment* and *sunk cost fallacy* make it seem as though you're being forced to continue with something harmful, something you wouldn't choose if you were to go back and choose again. And of course in some cases this is true, like when facing a hurtful relationship or declining stock portfolio. In these instances, your contributions may tie you to something that has a poor treasures-to-troubles ratio and is unlikely to improve.

But contributions are also a powerful, positive part of commitment. Contributions give you staying power. The more energy and resources you give to something meaningful, the more determined you'll be to follow through, even on the trying days. Without those contributions, you may quickly give up whenever things get hard. But contributions send you a powerful message: "Yes, there will be days when you don't want to keep going, days that are so frustrating you think about dropping your goal or making a dramatic exit. But you won't. You'll keep going. Not because of willpower and not because you're a saint. But because you will have contributed so much that you don't feel like you can quit." You don't have to be virtuous. You just have to be invested.

When you know how contributions work, you can more mindfully contribute to the areas of your life you find most meaningful, and pull back on the areas that no longer reflect what's most important to you. You can also assist others to increase commitment by inviting and valuing their contributions.

The Takeaway
Using Knowledge of Contributions to Affect Your Commitment Goals

All In

If you are interested in going all in, you'll benefit from increasing your contributions. Consider one or more of the following avenues for doing so.

- Contribute even when you don't feel like it. Often actions come first and feelings follow.

- Create "side bets" that make it more likely you will follow through. For example, tell people about your commitment (post it on Facebook, announce it at work).

- When you contribute, ask yourself how you feel. Notice the feelings of meaning and value that come from giving to this commitment.

Moving On

If you are interested in moving on, it's important to decrease your contributions. Consider one or more of the following avenues for starting the process to de-commit.

- Slowly start decreasing your contributions and see how that feels. Notice if it feels more meaningful to let go or switch gears for now.

- Set a limit on how much more you are willing to contribute before pulling out, and keep your word, as hard as it may be.

- Ask a trusted and objective third party to weigh in on whether your contributions are getting the payoff they should.

- Ask yourself if the value and meaning to be gained from staying will surpass the time, talent, tenderness, and tangibles you must still put in to make it work.

- Losing the resources you've already contributed can be hard. Reframe those investments and see them in a different way. For example, instead of "I wasted three years of my life at that job," say, "I got an invaluable education on what is important to me."

Assisting Others

If you are interested in assisting others to higher commitment, invite their contributions. Consider one or more of the following avenues for doing so.

- Observe how much others naturally contribute. This can be an indicator of their current level of commitment.

- Ask for small contributions before asking for larger contributions.

- Invite others to contribute as early in the process as possible.

- Always thank them for their contribution. They need to know how much you value their time, talent, tenderness, and/or tangibles.

- Be mindful that you continue to create an environment in which others have something to treasure. Otherwise they may be committed but not happy.

- Contribute at a high level yourself.

▪ CHAPTER 6 ▪

Choices: What Are Your Alternatives?

(Treasures – Troubles) + Contributions – Choices = Level of Commitment

Wᴀᴇɴ I met Melinda O'Malley Keckler, she was the five o'clock news anchor for Channel Two. It was her dream job, the one for which she'd gone to school, completed the internships, and taken the agonizing four a.m. shifts. All her years of training and fifteen years of working different time slots in multiple cities had finally paid off. Melinda treasured her job, everything from being on set and reading off the teleprompter to live reporting in the field and covering fascinating stories about interesting people in difficult situations. By comparison, the troubles of the career—like the long hours and inherent drama of live TV—were minor costs compared to all she treasured about her work and everything she'd contributed to make her dream a reality.

With the birth of her first child, however, came the initial feeling that something would have to change. Each time she left her daughter with the nanny and headed into the studio, she felt a pang of envy that someone else would get to spend those hours with her little girl. But because her work was rewarding, and because she'd made so many contributions to get where she was, she pushed through the feelings that she was missing out on something important. Then she gave birth to her second child. Her first child was now off to school each morning and the new arrival needed care. Melinda started to feel like she was "walking a tightrope" between her home life and her work life. "Some days the wind would blow and it would feel like I'm about ready to fall off," she recalls. But she walked that tightrope for two more years, feeling unbalanced and trying to make it all work. The major trouble was the two p.m. to eleven p.m. work hours associated with prime-time news. When Melinda could be at home, the kids were usually at school or fast asleep. After a while she couldn't ignore the empty feeling of being away from her children. The troubling aspects of her occupation were coming more clearly into view, and the joy of the position started falling away. She finally sat down with her husband to figure out what to do.

Melinda and her husband had many long talks about her predicament. They knew she had a rare and wonderful position, one that she had trained for specifically and that was unlikely to come around again. The family had come to depend on her income as well. It seemed as if she would have to stay, regardless of how she felt. But to her surprise, her husband eventually said something that significantly shifted her mind-set: "You know? Let's just let it go." In that moment, and in the days to come, Melinda's priorities changed.

Prior to that time, she hadn't realized she had a choice. Because her training was so specialized to TV journalism, she'd assumed success in a different career would be impossible. But a new awareness dawned on her: "The truth of the matter is, I can walk away. I can make things better." The recognition that she had a choice, and that nothing was actually stopping her, was exciting and empowering. Melinda decided to trust that she would find an acceptable alternative, and told the station she was leaving. "I felt certain I would land on my feet somehow. I'd seen other people leave the industry and do just fine."

At her next professional luncheon when the attendees were asked if anyone had an announcement, Melinda stood up and said, "I just want everyone to know that this is my last night on Channel Two. I don't know what else I'm doing yet. I'm taking a leap of faith. Just wanted you to know that's what's new with me." When she sat down, she could see the room was buzzing with whispered conversation. Melinda had been known as "the news lady" around town for years. It was hard for people to see her as anything else. But because of her announcement in this forum, she received her first job offer unrelated to the news studio. While it didn't seem all that sexy compared to being a news anchor, the part-time PR job with the Department of Correction had ideal hours and, more important, allowed for quality time with her children. Working at this job, Melinda realized her journalism skills transferred beautifully to other kinds of work. Writing press releases was easy after writing news stories, and no one had to tell her what a deadline meant.

Today Melinda has a full-time job at a university as the assistant director of marketing and communications. The university hired some serious talent, given the skills, enthusiasm, and professionalism Melinda brings. But she says she's the fortunate one. "It feels like my journalism career just set the table. It got me ready for the next step."

The Meaning of Choices

Our level of commitment is predicted by how much we treasure something, minus how troubling it is, plus the amount we've contributed, minus how much we see other good choices. Melinda treasured her work and she had contributed a great deal to her career. These two elements of the Commitment Equation kept her from considering other choices. But then things changed with the birth of her children, and the troubling aspects of her career came into view. She probably would have remained committed to her position as news anchor if she hadn't begun to wonder whether there was another choice, one that would allow her to use her talents and also raise her two children. If circumstances had been different, leaving her job wouldn't have been the better choice— for example, if she treasured advancing to a larger news market, or if leaving the job would irrevocably damage her family finances. But in Melinda's case, she saw she had a choice about changing gears and finding another fulfilling career, as her colleagues before her had done.

When we imagine other choices that might better meet our needs, our commitment tends to decline, as it did for Melinda. If we don't believe we have better alternatives to choose from, our commitment to where we are tends to be maintained or increased. While alternative choices may (or may not) be good for the individual, they are always "bad" for the current commitment. Consider the wife who develops a close, platonic friendship with another man, or the beloved college football coach who gets an offer to join the NFL. The new friendship or the NFL job might be a good opportunity for the wife or coach, but it poses a threat to the current commitment.

In this chapter we'll focus on how perceiving choices decreases commitment and ignoring choices increases commitment. Specifically, we'll consider the following:

1. Our imagination about choices negatively impacts commitment as much as (or more than) concrete choices do.
2. When we are highly committed, we ignore and devalue other choices.
3. When we wish to avoid commitment, we continually focus on other choices.
4. Sometimes it's in our best interest to consider other alternatives and make decisions that create new commitments.

Let's begin with the two kinds of choices that impact our level of commitment—concrete and imaginary choices.

Concrete Versus Imaginary Choices

Let's say you enjoy your job at a software design company, but then a friend invites you to become an owner in his smaller start-up. This is an example of a concrete choice. An actual, real-life option has opened up, and you must choose between staying in your current position and accepting your friend's offer and joining the new firm as an owner. As you ponder your choice, one of three things will happen. One possibility is you'll realize your current job meets your needs well and you'll remain committed. Your commitment might even increase if you recognize you have a great job doing what you love without any personal financial risk. A second possibility is the new choice reveals what's missing in your current job, say autonomy and control or the opportunity to take the company in an exciting direction. Staying where you are may still be the best choice, but because you've contemplated what you're missing, your enthusiasm and commitment to your current job decline. A third possibility is the new opportunity seems far superior to what you are currently doing, and your commitment to your job takes a dive. You tell your boss you quit, and you join your friend in a new venture. If this concrete choice had not emerged, you may have continued at your job without a second thought.

But sometimes we compare our current situation to what we expect or *imagine* we could get somewhere else. When Melinda decided to leave her job she didn't have a concrete alternative just yet, but she imagined there had to be something out there that would better meet her needs. Have you ever been in a relationship and thought, "I don't have any other options right now, but there has to be something better than this"? If so, you were comparing the low level of satisfaction you felt in the current relationship with the satisfaction you believed you deserved and imagined you could gain from an as yet unknown alternative.

This may seem surprising, but the research suggests that imaginary choices decrease commitment as much as concrete choices do. We've all seen the guy who thinks he has lots of options in the dating world, and his belief—right or wrong—keeps him from investing in any one person. We've probably also seen the guy who remains in a terrible relationships longer than he should because he imagines he'll never find anything better. In both cases, it isn't necessarily the *reality* of choices that's affecting his commitment, but his *beliefs* about reality.

Where do imaginary choices come from? You may recall from Chapter 2 that we discussed the work of social psychologists John Thibaut and Harold Kelley. Thibaut and Kelley theorized that people develop close relationships when rewards outweigh costs, and when their satisfaction is greater in their current relationship than what they believe they could get elsewhere. The way we decide whether our relationship is better than what we could get elsewhere is through comparison. We compare the treasures and troubles of this relationship (or job or project) to another concrete choice or to our general expectations about how meaningful and enjoyable a relationship should be. This comparison level comes, in part, from past personal experience. For example, if you've done a lot of previous volunteer work that's been exceptionally rewarding, you will have a fairly high comparison level for your current volunteer activity. If your current volunteer job meets this level, you are likely to stay with it. But if it falls short, you may want to leave—not because you have a concrete alternative right now, but because you believe there are generally better volunteer opportunities out there.

In addition to past experience, our comparison level is influenced by what we see in the media. Nearly four hundred married people were asked about their TV viewing habits and their relationship commitment for a study published in the journal *Mass Communication and Society*. On average, the people in the study had been married for nineteen years, and they spent about half of their TV viewing time on shows with "romantic themes." Programs from medical dramas to dating games, soap operas to reality shows include themes of love and human bonding. The question posed by the researcher was, "Do these shows increase the perception that we have lots of other attractive choices for partners?" Indeed, that turned out to be the case. Generally speaking, the more hours of romantically themed television the participants watched, the more likely they were to believe they had good alternatives to their marriage, and the lower their commitment to their marriage. However, the act of viewing these shows didn't harm commitment as much as *believing* that the relationships portrayed on TV are accurate. People who watched a lot of this media and believed the portrayals were a fair comparison for their relationship were less committed. For those who did not believe the portrayals were realistic, watching more hours didn't lead to less commitment. It appears that if you believe the experience of *The Bachelor* is accurate, you imagine a world with a lot of wonderful romantic options. And as such, there's no need to get overly attached to your current partner.

Researchers at Florida State University found a similar result for pornography. They asked men and women who regularly viewed pornography to stop for three weeks. Afterward, they measured their level of relationship commitment and compared it with that of a group who had not been asked to curb their consumption. The first group—the participants who temporarily removed or reduced their use of pornography—ended up significantly more committed to their relationship. There was nothing else different between these two groups. All it took to increase commitment was to avoid looking at other naked ladies or guys (the findings applied to both men and women). In a follow-up study, the researchers found that people who viewed pornography more frequently were also more likely to cheat on their partner. Regular viewing of attractive people having sex appears to create a perception of a world with lots of seemingly available partners. If you expect to have abundant choices, you'll be less devoted to what you already have.

Concrete and imaginary choices also affect our commitment to brands. Let's take the example of how committed you are to your bank. Certainly, a large degree of your satisfaction and commitment comes from how your bank performs. At some level you have evaluated the bank's service: the degree to which the tellers are friendly, how easy it is to get a loan, and whether they have the particular financial options you need. But the performance of your bank isn't all that matters. Marketing researchers tell us that our satisfaction is also influenced by whether the bank (or any brand) performs at a higher level than we expect from that brand. They call this *expectancy disconfirmation*. If you hear from all your friends that this brand is really great, only to find it is so-so, your satisfaction will be lower than if you'd gone in with neutral expectations. We can say that satisfaction with a brand is based on performance plus the degree to which performance exceeds or falls below expectations. Of course, what we really care about is commitment. We know that someone may be satisfied with their bank and leave anyway, and another may stay with their bank even when they're dissatisfied. Clearly, something besides the bank's ability to meet their needs is driving these decisions. What matters for commitment, according to the experiments of marketing researchers Kamal Gupta and David Stewart, is not that the bank exceeds what is expected of the brand. It's not even that it exceeds a competing brand. What matters for commitment is that it exceeds expectations about banks in general, the mental picture we have about how they are supposed to operate.

One of the mechanisms through which these mental pictures and expectations are developed is advertising. Advertising can be very effective at encouraging people to purchase a product, but it may also create unrealistic expectations about what products can do for us, similar to the way romantic-themed television and pornography can affect our expectations about relationships. If your expectation about a category of product is elevated to unrealistic heights, you may find yourself moving from brand to brand, hoping you'll finally find one that lives up to the hype. How many women have at least four brands of lipstick in their cosmetics drawer, for example? When our expectations have been so highly elevated, it's hard to admit that no lipstick stays for eight hours, no antiperspirant stops heavy sweat, and no pill removes ten pounds from your waistline in a week. The downside of unrealistic advertising is we can end up less committed to the brands we use, looking for another option that does all it promises.

If you have a goal that involves going all in or assisting others to higher commitment it's important to establish realistic expectations. It's certainly tempting, if you want people to buy your product, join your team, or take a job at your company, to tell them it will be the best experience of their lives. The problem surfaces when you can't live up to those expectations, and those same people become dissatisfied and less committed. Coach Chris Petersen is always direct and honest with potential college football recruits. He tells them what they can expect on his team, particularly how difficult and demanding it will be. The last thing he wants, he says, is for a guy to join the team and then end up quitting due to unmet expectations. Setting realistic expectations is a key component to commitment and the overall success of the team.

As a consumer of media, it's important to recognize the images you see and the messages you hear that can subtly increase your expectations and lead you to believe there are many attractive alternatives that will bring you satisfaction. What's even more important is whether you believe what you see. You can consume romantic media without harming your commitment, for example, if you remind yourself it isn't real and doesn't reflect a concrete choice. "For entertainment purposes only," as they say. If you know you are susceptible to what you see in the media, however, you may want to avoid too much sexy and romantic stuff in the first place in order to stay focused on your commitment.

Commitment is based in part on whether you believe you have other good alternatives to choose from—choices that would bring more satisfaction than what you are committed to now. Sometimes your commitment competes with a concrete choice and sometimes it competes with the imaginary choices based on past experience and what you see in the media. Concrete and imaginary choices aren't necessarily good or bad. They can be good if you wish to leave your current commitment or bad if you wish to stay with it. If you have a commitment goal of moving on, it's important to open your mind to the possibility that there are other options for you, just as Melinda did when she realized her job as a news anchor was keeping her from her children. Even if you don't see a concrete choice, if you believe there is another way, you will likely find it. If you want to go all in, however, do what the highly committed do and avoid focusing on your other choices, concrete or imaginary.

Choice and Maintaining Commitment

Commitment is maintained when you take actions to keep it strong. We discussed one of these actions in the previous chapter—making contributions. When you contribute to a relationship, career, or project, your dedication steadily grows. The same can be said of ignoring your other choices. To maintain a desired commitment, you must focus on that commitment, rather than on the options. Your attention is meaningful. You may think there's no harm in perusing the Monster.com website just to see what other job opportunities are out there. You may think it's a good idea to ponder future projects while working on the current one. You may think "checking out" people besides your partner poses no threat to your relationship. But these distractions can work against you. What you focus your attention on matters. Focus on your commitment and it will grow. Focus on your other options and they will distract you from your current commitment. People with high commitment know this intuitively. They're not distracted by other options.

Ignoring Choices

Psychologist Rowland Miller invited people into the lab for what they thought was a study of "effectiveness in print advertising." Men and women, all in heterosexual relationships, viewed twelve slides of magazine ads for various products. Some of these slides featured attractive female models, some contained attractive male models, and some showed a product with no model. Imagine you're in this study, checking out these ads at your own pace, and unbeknownst to you the researcher is timing how long you look at each slide. If you look at the underwear model ad three times longer than the blender ad, Miller will know. Miller also has data, from a previous study, on how committed you are to your relationship, and he's making some interesting connections. When Miller examined the data he found that people with high commitment spent less time looking at the photos of attractive opposite-sex people. They looked only as long as they needed to evaluate the ad, and then moved on. Relatively speaking, the people with lower commitment took their time on those opposite-sex photos. Miller also found that the people who were more committed and who spent less time looking at the photos were more likely to be in the same relationship two months later. No surprise there—when we're more committed we're more likely to stay in the relationship. But here's the surprise: By looking at the amount of time they spent on the photos, Miller was able to predict whether they would stay together *just as well* as when he looked at whether they rated themselves as highly committed. Staying together could be predicted by perceived commitment level, but it could be equally predicted by the amount of attention paid to other attractive choices.

For good or for bad, anytime you ignore other alternatives you'll feel more dedicated to what you have. If you want to be highly committed, there is wisdom in not having a Plan B. As my friend Hannah said as she left to pursue her dreams of acting in Los Angeles, "If you have a Plan B you will probably take it." She wouldn't allow herself to imagine doing something else one day. If she did, she said, when things got tough, she would remember she had another option. "When things get bad, you can just drop out. But if you don't have a Plan B, if you decide this is it and this is your only choice, you have to make it work. You will stick it out and keep going. It's the only way to succeed in a business this hard." At first Hannah's theory sounded crazy to me. We all know the odds are weighted against most actors seeking bright lights and success in the entertainment industry. Actors have the highest unemployment rate after plasterers and mobile home installers. But it turns out Hannah is spot on when it comes to commitment. One of the best ways to remain committed when things get tough is to take away your other options. Or if you do see other good choices, devalue them.

Devaluing Choices

Imagine you are asked to provide feedback on a new online dating service. Part of your job is to evaluate the profile of one of the site's users. The developers know you are in a relationship and not looking for a date, though if you decide at a later time to use their service, they'll keep the information you provide to match you with potential candidates. You are given a photo of a physically attractive person of the other sex. There is also some information about this person, who is described as relatively happy, relaxed, and sincere. Now you are asked to rate the desirability of the candidate. What is your impression of his intelligence and humor, for example? How compatible, faithful, and supportive do you think he would be as a partner?

This was the setup of a psychological study at the University of North Carolina. The researchers wanted to know whether evaluations of the applicant would vary based on how committed the evaluator was to his or her current relationship. Indeed, those who had high levels of commitment gave significantly lower ratings to the attractive potential date. The researchers called this phenomenon the *devaluing of alternative partners*, and it has been replicated in many studies since then. Devaluing alternative partners is a primary way we keep our relationship commitment strong. The lower rating isn't something we just tell our partners to make them feel better. Devaluing alternatives is an internal process—a habit of perception—that serves to maintain commitment. The effect here seems to be circular, similar to how contributions affect commitment. Ignoring or disparaging alternatives increases our commitment, and higher levels of commitment lead to ignoring or disparaging alternatives.

Unfortunately, there is a risk in trying to get other people to

ignore or devalue their options. If this process isn't internally motivated, it can have the opposite effect. A team of researchers headed
by C. Nathan DeWall, of the University of Kentucky, ran a series
of experimental tests with people in heterosexual relationships.
Some participants were given an "attention task" that subtly required them to look away from images of attractive opposite-sex
people. Other participants did an attention task that didn't require
them to look away. After engaging in the task, the "look away"
participants actually had better memories of the attractive faces.
They also spent more time looking at attractive opposite-sex photos
in a follow-up task and reported less commitment to their existing
relationship. They were even more likely to have a favorable attitude
toward infidelity after this task. The authors dubbed this the Forbidden Fruit Hypothesis and suggested that when we tell someone
that something is off-limits, they will desire it even more. If a person is internally motivated to avoid cheese fries, for example, forc-
ing her away from them could undermine her internal motivation.
So, it appears, avoiding and devaluing other choices works best
when it's based on free will. Otherwise, you run the risk of making
the alternatives seem more enticing. Rather than attempting to control others, a better strategy is to pay attention to how interested
they appear in other options, as this can be a fair indicator of their
current commitment. Indeed, as you are about to see, focusing on
choices is one of the ways people evade commitment.

Choice and Evading Commitment

Like most newlyweds, my husband and I needed to buy furniture
for our new home. In particular, we really needed a sofa. I wasn't

too picky—my main concern was comfort. My husband, Jeff, an interior design nut, wanted to identify the perfect couch for our mid-century modern home. So for an extended period of time we considered our options. We looked through magazines and catalogs and searched online sources. We visited showrooms in several cities. And after months of searching and deliberating, we found a sofa we thought would meet our needs. Unfortunately, we had to wait a few more months for the sofa to be manufactured and delivered. Finally the day came and the new sofa arrived. I was ecstatic to have a place to sit. It was beautiful and comfortable, and quickly became my favorite spot in the house. My husband wasn't as excited. "We should have gone with a smaller scale, and we should have gone with leather," he said, eying the sofa skeptically. It had just arrived and already it wasn't right.

You see, I married a *maximizer*—someone who doesn't look for good or great, but who looks for optimal. If it isn't the best possible choice, it doesn't deserve the maximizer's acceptance, or commitment. It's not that maximizers are afraid of commitment. It's that their drive for optimal decisions makes it difficult to enjoy and commit to what they have.

How much of a maximizer are you? Consider how much you agree with these statements taken from the maximization scale developed by psychologist Barry Schwartz and his colleagues: "I never settle for second best"; "Whenever I'm faced with a choice, I try to imagine what all the other possibilities are, even ones that aren't present at the moment"; "No matter what I do, I have the highest standards for myself." Would you say you completely agree, completely disagree, or something in between? People who score low on the maximization scale are referred to as *satisficers*. Satisficers stop looking at their options when they find a good choice. Their goal is finding something that satisfies their need rather than finding the best option possible.

Consider this example based on an experiment by Erin Sparks and her colleagues at Florida State University. Imagine you are asked to rate how much you like fifteen posters. They include images of movies and musicians, famous paintings and big cities. You are given a stack of fifteen eight-by-eleven-inch prints that represent the posters, and you begin sorting them by most to least favorite. Maybe you decide your favorite is the Jimi Hendrix poster, followed by a Maui beach scene, and you continue to rate them all the way down to a replica of the *Mona Lisa*. You do a few other tasks, and before you go, the researchers tell you some of the prints are available as full posters. They'd like to give you one to take, so you look at the available options. They are all posters in the middle of your rankings. Of those, you select a decent poster, maybe a cityscape of New York City. Next, the researchers tell you that preferences can change over time, and they'd like you to rate the fifteen posters one more time, reflecting how you feel right now. They also want to know how satisfied you are with the poster you decided to take.

A week later the experimenters contact you. They ask about your satisfaction with the poster now, and they want to know what you did with it. Did you keep it or give it away? If you kept it, did you put it on your wall or toss it to the back of a closet? In short, they wish to determine how committed you became to the poster after you selected it.

We'll get to the study results in a moment, but first consider other decisions we might make in a day. We could select a sofa, for example, or a place to live or work. We might select a long-term project to pursue. Whatever you are selecting, the question is, once you make that decision, will you commit to it and be happy with it even if you know there's likely a better option out there somewhere, even if it isn't a concrete choice now?

When put into the same situation—selecting a poster from several that weren't ideal—maximizers and satisficers responded differently. Those who scored high on maximizing were much less satisfied with the poster they chose. They were more likely to give it away or toss it in a closet, indicating a low level of investment or attachment. Meanwhile, those who scored low on maximizing were pretty happy with what they got and were more likely to display their poster on a wall. Recall that researchers had the participants re-rank the fifteen posters after they selected one, to see if their preferences had changed. People who scored low on maximizing were more likely to adjust their rankings and gave the poster they selected a higher ranking. For example, if they'd originally ranked the New York cityscape at number six, they might have moved it up to number three after becoming its owner.

This adjustment is psychologically beneficial and comes quite naturally for many of us. For example, perhaps you had a hard time deciding which dog to choose at the pound, but once you picked one you became certain you'd made the right choice. You see Einstein as a wonderful companion even though he chews the fur off his own tail. If you weren't certain of your choice, you'd continue to think about the dogs you passed over and even other, imaginary dogs that weren't at the pound that day. You'd focus on Einstein's bald tail and experience distress and internal conflict. That's what can happen when we aren't truly committed to what we have. Psychologists call it *cognitive dissonance*. One of the benefits of commitment is the reduction of cognitive dissonance. We stop comparing and contrasting our various options and we focus on what we have. But people who score high on the maximization scale don't realize this benefit. Presumably, they think they'll be happier and more satisfied if they remain available for something better. Committing to a choice takes that possibility off the table. The irony is that in the search for the optimal choice, along with the avoidance of committing to anything less, maximizers are less satisfied with the choices they do make. As Socrates said, "He who is not contented with what he has would not be contented with what he would like to have."

Of course, we aren't talking about when you are truly unhappy with something in your life. If a job is causing you a lot of trouble and there's not much to treasure, that's different. That's the time to explore your other options. We're talking about those times when we discount the good in our lives and become unwilling to embrace it because we feel if we looked hard enough, we could find something better.

My research assistant, Kristine, refers to this phenomenon as *future surfing*. We're thinking about all the potential things that could happen in the future. "What if I find someone better? What if I realize this is the wrong place to live? What if something goes wrong at this job?" Surfing the future for all possibilities keeps us from making commitments. We can end up investing more of our time and energy in the imagined what-ifs than in the reality of right now. How about we set aside those what-ifs and make the most of what we have? If you give your attention and energy to a commitment and it still isn't right, at least you'll know you made an effort. You'll be able to walk away with confidence and let go of the what-ifs.

Perhaps it's clear that if you want to let go of a commitment— that is, to avoid being psychologically attached to something with the intent to stay with it—refocusing your attention on your other choices is a good way to do it. Of course, it might appear to outsiders that you are afraid of commitment.

Commitment Phobia

As popular as the phrase is, there is technically no such thing as "commitment phobia." An investigation of the *Diagnostic and Statistical Manual of Mental Disorders* (DSM) will show phobias ranging from snakes to planes to snakes *on* planes, but nothing about commitment. That's because what looks like a fear of commitment in relationships is really a fear of dependence, connection, and vulnerability, a fear of getting "lost" in another person only to have him or her fail to meet your needs. And if that's your vision of a relationship, it's no wonder you want to avoid it. These kinds of fears are believed to come from early childhood experiences with a primary caregiver that led to a particular attachment style. (We discussed attachment styles briefly in Chapter 1.) Roughly 20 percent of the population has what is called an *avoidant* attachment style.

Imagine that Jasper has been dating the same woman for several years, but he never lets her get too close. His friends and family always talk about the importance of commitment and dedication, but it goes right over Jasper's head. Being committed means being open and vulnerable to another person, something Jasper has no interest in. In fact, to keep an emotional buffer between himself and his partner, he likes reading the singles ads and imagining the women he could meet and date if he were on his own. Whenever he goes out of town for work, he stays out late and flirts with the women he meets in the bars. Of course, he doesn't tell his partner about these things—in fact, he doesn't tell her much of anything.

Why does he behave this way? People like Jasper (or Jennifer—the number of men and women with an avoidant attachment style is about fifty-fifty) likely got an unflattering picture of close relationships at an early age. While avoidant types may look tough and independent, they need closeness and affirmation as much as the rest of us. But because they didn't experience that kind of relating in their youth, they don't have a mental picture of what it looks like or how to experience it. As children they had a relatively weak bond with their primary caregiver. They interacted with her or him in essentially the same way they interacted with a stranger. When she was absent and then returned, they didn't feel particularly comforted. Their caregiver tended to be disengaged and unresponsive, and as children they learned that others are not to be counted on and are unlikely to meet their needs.

Once this picture of close relationships is developed, it tends to be replicated in adult relationships. You can think of it like a self-fulfilling prophecy. If you expect a relationship will be troubling and unfulfilling, and that it will ultimately fail, you're more likely to behave in a manner that will bring about its demise. Indeed, study after study shows that people with an avoidant attachment style have lower levels of commitment and satisfaction in their relationships, and they experience more breakups. Let's look at an example.

Researchers from McGill University developed a list of the common positive events that can happen in the course of a developing relationship and that increase commitment, like beginning to date exclusively or deciding to spend your lives together. They also developed a list of common negative events that undermine commitment, like falling out of love or becoming interested in someone else. The combination of events you expect to happen in a relationship creates your relationship map. The researchers reasoned that people with an avoidant style would expect more negative events. Their map of a typical relationship might be, "You begin to spend more time together, then problems of past relationships come up, and one of you realizes you're no longer interested." Meanwhile, the map of a person with a more secure attachment style might be, "You start to trust your partner, decide to date exclusively, discuss your future together, and get engaged." Indeed, that's what the researchers found.

Statistically, having an avoidant attachment style was associated with expectations of experiencing negative, commitment-harming events (and not enhancing events) as well as expectations of relationship failure. Their relationship maps have many potholes and dead ends, and few easy, scenic drives. Is it any wonder they avoid contributing to a relationship and work instead to keep their options open? Is it any wonder they'd rather choose to go it alone than maneuver through the many perceived negative events that will only lead to failure? Sadly, it is this pessimistic belief that keeps the commitment avoidant types from experiencing something different and better.

As we've seen, one of the most straightforward ways to keep commitment low is to focus on other options, and psychologists from three universities showed that's what avoidant types tend to do. People who scored high on avoidant attachment were more likely to check out people of the opposite sex and to hold their gaze for longer periods. They were also more likely to cheat on their partners.

So let's review. People with an avoidant attachment style tend to keep their distance in relationships. They do this because they have an internal map that suggests their relationships will not be fulfilling and instead will be littered with harmful events that take away from commitment and satisfaction. Given their map, people with an avoidant attachment style may behave in a manner that resembles commitment phobia. One of the ways they demonstrate their aversion to commitment is by keeping their options open. Rather than focusing on and nurturing the relationship they're in, they regularly check out their options and may even engage in extracurricular sexual activity. They end up with a self-fulfilling prophecy; that is, they create the very sort of relationship they expected—one that disappoints and doesn't last.

Unfortunately, avoiding commitment doesn't end with relationships. People with an avoidant attachment style report lower levels of commitment to their organizations as well and have a greater intention to quit. Since this is a relatively new area of research, we don't know why this is, but it may have something to do with how avoidant people approach professional goals. According to two leading experts on attachment styles, Mario Mikulincer and Phillip Shaver, avoidant people are less committed to pursuing challenging goals and are less willing to ask for support. As a result, they tend to give up easily when encountering relatively minor difficulties and defensively withdraw from difficult tasks.

It's not all bad news, however. First, to those of you who may avoid commitment in relationships or jobs, it may be because you haven't found the right person or profession. Let's not get ahead of ourselves. But if you identify with the other aspects of avoidant attachment—believing people aren't to be trusted and challenging goals aren't worth it—it may be time to acknowledge you have a mental map that isn't helping you get what you want. While you can't change the way you were raised or the inclination toward an attachment style that came from your past, you can be aware of your tendencies today and choose new behaviors. Just because something feels natural, like keeping others at a distance or avoiding difficult challenges at work, doesn't mean you have to do it. If you want to go all in at work, it's helpful to change your behavior when it comes to asking for support. If you are staunchly self-reliant, asking for help may feel like a poke in the eye with a sharp stick, but getting the support you need may be the difference between quitting and following through. If you want to go all in in a relationship, remember that a fear of commitment is not really a fear of commitment. It might be the fear of being too vulnerable, the fear of not getting your needs met, or the fear of being let down. As you create some positive relationship experiences you will begin to see that some people (especially people with a secure attachment style) are able to have a balanced relationship in which both people's needs are met without anyone feeling as if they are disappearing into the other person.

If you are in a relationship with someone who appears to avoid commitment, you may wonder if it's possible to have an assisting others goal under these circumstances. I'll be direct—it's difficult. It's much easier to generate devotion in someone who wants to be committed. If the relationship has value to you, it's worth trying a few things. First, you can serve as a model for what secure attachment looks like. As you demonstrate your trust and support, his tendencies toward avoidance may begin to subside, especially over time as you repeatedly reaffirm that trust and support. If you are willing to do the work, he may begin to open up to greater vulnerability and commitment. Monitor his willingness to contribute to the relationship and try to determine whether he is truly open to change. Otherwise, your contributions will be serving to increase your own commitment and not his.

Choosing a New Commitment

If you want to increase commitment in your life, the message from social science research is clear: Stay focused on what's important and devalue your other options, concrete or imaginary. When you identify a valuable goal, project, or relationship, avoid the temptation to constantly try to "trade up." Contribute to what matters most and ignore the rest.

What research can't tell you is whether or not a particular commitment is right for you. That's for you to decide. In some cases you'll realize, like Melinda did, that a commitment no longer meets your needs or reflects your values. It's not that you weren't invested, and it's not that you were looking around at your options. It's that you started to get the sense that something wasn't right or you weren't where you were supposed to be. You may have even felt guilty for having that thought. The commitment was a part of you for so long, how could you consider going somewhere else, doing something else, or experiencing something else? You may have resisted looking at your other choices because it felt like a betrayal.

The question to ask when you feel this internal conflict is one only you can answer: "What am I really committed to?" We rarely ask that question, and yet the answer is often within us if we take the time to ask. It may be that you don't have to leave a commitment as much as *change its form*. Kristine, whom you met at the beginning of Chapter 4, changed the form of her commitment to her family and religion. First, she needed to determine what she was really committed to. Was it the institute of marriage and following the church bylaws? Was it her desire to be a great mom and to nurture a happy, healthy relationship with her partner, married or not? When she realized it was the latter, she was able to adjust the form of her commitments to what really mattered to her.

Melinda was able to answer the same question. Once she realized that spending quality time with her children was more important to her than her position as a news anchor, and once she realized she would have alternative job opportunities, she was able to let go of her former commitment. Now she is committed to her new occupation, utilizing her talents in a different context. And she has more time with her family. Melinda didn't take a totally different path that required a new education and an altered skill set (although she told me she admires people who do that too). She answered the most important question she could ask herself and then realigned her commitment around the answer.

Focusing on alternative choices can be harmful to an important commitment. But in other cases, seeking alternatives is the right choice when you are committed to something that's no longer in your best interest. The key is to approach or avoid choices consciously based on what's truly important to you. The husband who wants to be committed to his wife isn't doing himself any favors by habitually checking out other women and imagining them as potential partners. And the employee who is unhappy with her job isn't doing herself any favors by habitually ignoring other employment options. The first choice to make is whether to explore or ignore your alternatives. And this choice is within your control.

At this point, you should have a great understanding of how the four elements work together to predict levels of commitment. Those elements are treasures, troubles, contributions, and choices, and a change in one influences the others. For example, when what you treasure about a relationship increases, you may begin to ignore your other choices. And when you ignore your other choices, you will probably contribute more to the relationship you have. Or if you are always looking at other careers, you may not contribute as much to the job you have, and because you're not contributing as much as you could, it may seem your career has more troubles than treasures. You can't control all of the circumstances that influence whether you or someone else will have a high or low level of commitment. But there is always something you can do that will make a difference. If you understand what drives commitment, you can direct your focus and your efforts in ways that allow you to make adjustments to reach your goals. Don't take commitment for granted. It's too important to your well-being. Decide what you value, choose your commitments consciously, and employ what you know about the equation to make it happen.

The Takeaway
Using Knowledge of Choices to Affect Your Commitment Goals

All In

If you are interested in going all in, you will benefit from focusing on your commitment rather than on your choices. Consider one or more of the following avenues for doing so.

- Reduce how frequently you search for other concrete options.
- Reduce how frequently you indulge yourself in imagining other options.

- Focus on making a good choice, rather than a maximizing choice.

- Be aware of when you are "future surfing," and bring your attention back to the choice in front of you now.

- Identify what you value prior to choosing.

- If fear of commitment is stopping you, identify what you are actually afraid of. Be willing to change your mental map.

Moving On

If you are interested in moving on, it will help to investigate new options. Consider one or more of the following avenues for starting the process to de-commit.

- Don't let the current lack of a concrete option keep you from imagining other choices.

- Brainstorm other options that still reflect your values.

- Ask, "What am I really committed to?" Think about whether there is an alternative way that commitment can be expressed.

- Believe. Trust you will find your way.

Assisting Others

If you are interested in assisting others, be aware that choices are the element of the equation over which you have the least influence. However, consider one or more of the following avenues for helping others who seem to avoid commitment.

- Pay attention to whether they are looking at other choices, since that's an indicator of reduced commitment.

- Determine if a commitment avoider wants to change.

- Help out the maximizer by offering a limited number of choices.

- Don't try to prevent others from looking at their choices, as that can encourage them.

· PART III ·

Engaging the Commitment Equation

*W*elcome to your action plan, where you are invited to develop a plan for a commitment goal. Use Chapter 7, "All In," to create a plan for using the commitment elements to increase your commitment. Use Chapter 8, "Moving On," to make small changes that help with letting go of a commitment. Use Chapter 9, "Assisting Others," to make adjustments that will help others be more committed. While you may not be able to impact all four of the areas that affect commitment—treasures, troubles, contributions, and choices—even a small change in one area can affect the whole equation.

Reading through the action plan chapters will clarify the ideas in this book and help you understand how you can use them in a specific situation in your life. Of course, real change will happen when you get out a pen and paper, follow the writing prompts, and take action.

▪ CHAPTER 7 ▪

All In

THIS chapter outlines the action plan for increasing commitment in an important area of your life. Maybe it's time to dedicate yourself to a professional goal, or perhaps you want to strengthen your commitment to a relationship. Your commitment will be stronger when you focus on treasures and contributions and pay less attention to troubles and choices, and in this section you'll create an action plan to do just that. This may be a lot to do all at once, so begin with one or two steps and work through the chapter slowly. For each step, you'll see an example of someone who wants to commit to regular exercise. Think of this as an example only. Your action plan will look different because you and your situation are unique.

Step One: Define Your Commitment

Begin by identifying what you want to be committed to and why. It's good to be as specific as possible, using details that will help you vividly imagine what the commitment looks like. Being concrete will also help you track your progress. I'll show an example first, and then it's your turn. Be sure to have pen and paper handy.

- The What: I want to be committed to working out regularly by going to the gym at least three times a week for a minimum of forty-five minutes.
- The Why: I want to have more energy and less stress, and feel stronger and leaner.

Now it's your turn: *What do you want to be more committed to, and why?*

Step Two: Reflect on Treasures

Even though you aren't fully committed yet, there are things about this activity or relationship you value. Make a list of the things you currently treasure about this commitment, including both the big and the small. Nothing is too small if you find it rewarding. In the workout example, someone might list these as current treasures:

- Feeling energized and strong after the workout.
- Connecting with others who care about their health.
- Fitting into the clothes I used to wear.
- Listing to music while working out.
- Feeling good about myself.

It's your turn: *What do you currently treasure about your commitment, including the big and small?*

Now, what new treasures could you add to the equation? What could you do differently, or what could you ask for, that would make this commitment more worthwhile, fun, or valuable? Big things are great and little things count too; everything goes into the equation. Be as specific as you can. Continuing the workout example:

- I could add a trainer to keep me motivated.
- I could add some new music to my MP3 player.
- I could find an activity that's really fun.

Your turn: *What new treasures could you add to the equation? What could you do differently, or what could you ask for, large and small?*

Step Three: Increase Treasures

Now that you know what you find rewarding, it's time to take full advantage of those treasures.

Take the items from your *current* treasures list and write them on an index card. Carry these treasures with you for a few days to remind yourself of what you value about this commitment. If or when your commitment begins to wane, refer to this list.

For each of the *new* treasures you listed, write out what you will do and by when to begin creating that treasure. Be specific. For example:

- For the music treasure, I will use the iTunes Genius feature to find some new songs. I will purchase at least five new ones tonight.

- For the treasure about finding an activity that's really fun, I will try out two new classes within the next week, even the classes that look weird or intimidating, like the Zumba class and the karate class.

Your turn: *What step will you take to begin creating each treasure, and by when?*

Write a letter to your future self, the one who is fully committed and is enjoying the outcomes of this commitment. In the letter, tell your future self how proud you are of him or her, and describe what life is like and the treasures you have as a result of this commitment. As you write, really see this and believe it. (Bonus: It's fun to read the letter after you really have created this!) For the workout example:

> Dear Self,
>
> Congratulations on being so committed to working out. Because of your commitment, exercise is more fun than ever before. Best of all, after every workout, you have more energy than you did before you started, and you've made some great new friends—people who also want to be healthy and whom you can count on to keep you on track. I also want to emphasize how easy it was! . . .

Your turn: *Write a letter to your future self. Include the treasures you have as a result of this commitment. Write as though it's already happened and you are feeling great about following though with your commitment.*

Step Four: Identify Troubles

As much as you want this commitment and value what it will bring to your life, there is something holding you back: the troubles. We're going to identify them and see which ones can be reduced.

What are the troubles of this commitment? What is the downside that makes you think twice about staying with it? Like treasures, no trouble is too small to put on the list, because any trouble removed will help the whole equation. List them all, even the ones you may be just imagining. Our committed exerciser might write:

- The gym is huge and I feel lost.
- The parking is horrible. Sometimes I have to drive around for over 15 minutes.
- It costs $45 a month to belong, which is kind of expensive.
- Everybody looks so fit that I feel uncomfortable.

Which of these are acceptable troubles to you (simply the "price of admission"), and which are troubles you'd really like to see changed, if possible? Create two lists. For example:

- Acceptable Troubles: Paying $45 a month, and feeling uncomfortable around superfit people.
- Troubles I'd Like to Change: Feeling lost in the huge gym, and the parking situation.

Your turn: *Which of these are acceptable troubles, and which are troubles you'd like to change?*

Step Five: Decrease Troubles

For each trouble you'd like to change, brainstorm ways you could lessen the trouble. Feel free to come up with wild ideas—anything you think might ease the trouble. Think of actions you could take yourself, and think of things you could ask for. For example:

- The gym is huge and I feel lost.

    I could get to know one trainer.

    I could consistently go to the same class so I get to know some of the people better.

    I could join a smaller gym.

    I could order gym equipment and work out in my garage.

- The parking is horrible.

    I could play a motivational CD in the car while looking for a parking spot.

    I could splurge on reserved parking.

    I could join a smaller gym.

    I could take the bus/ride a bike/carpool with a friend.

Your turn: *What could you do to ease each trouble? This is the brainstorming phase, so put down whatever comes to you, no limits. What could you do, or what could you ask for?*

Which of the solutions do you think might work? Write down one or two you are willing to try, along with a deadline. If the solution has several steps, identify each step, with deadlines. For example:

- By Tuesday, I will start a trial membership at the little club down the street. If I like it (and if I don't feel lost and the parking is good), I will switch.

Your turn: *What one or two solutions are you willing to try? Include any steps, with deadlines.*

As you can see, there are things you can do to increase treasures and decrease troubles. Even small adjustments can make you more satisfied, and satisfaction is a primary predictor of commitment. Now we'll move to the second half of the equation, where we'll make it easier for you to remain committed, even on your unhappy days.

Step Six: Acknowledge Contributions

Remember that commitments often "grow legs," and this process begins when you make contributions. Write an inventory of what you have already put into this commitment. Think of all four categories: time (days, years, energy), talent (skills, creativity), tenderness (sharing yourself, emotional investment), and tangibles (money, material items). Our exerciser's inventory might read:

- I have been paying $45 a month in fees for the past year.
- I bought some new cross-training shoes.
- I have met a few nice people who seem to care if I show up.
- I have put a lot of time and energy into learning some new weight routines.

Your turn: *What have you already put into this commitment in terms of time, talent, tenderness, and/or tangibles?*

As you look at your list, realize that in many ways this commitment is already a part of you. *Acknowledge yourself for all you have already contributed.*

Step Seven: Add Contributions

The more you invest, the more committed you're likely to be. What new contributions can you make in the form of time, talent, tenderness, and/or tangibles? In some cases, you might want to include a side bet; that is, to involve something or someone from the outside that leads you to follow through. Write a list of ideas for what you can do to increase the sense that you can't back out. Here's our exerciser:

- I can join the boot camp and prepay.
- I can post my goal on Facebook and continue sharing with follow-up posts.
- Whenever I leave the club, I can say to the gal at the front desk, "See you tomorrow."

Your turn: *What new contributions can you make in terms of time, talent, tenderness, and/or tangibles? Or what kind of side bet can you make?*

Of your ideas, identify one or more that you are willing to do right away, and give yourself a deadline. For example:

- I'll sign up for boot camp before the end of the month.
- Immediately thereafter, I'll announce it on Facebook.

You turn: *Which of your ideas are you going to do right away, and by when?*

Step Eight: Manage Choices

One of the reasons you aren't as committed as you want is that you've been considering other choices. This section is about helping you focus on your commitment, rather than on your options.

Write an inventory of the alternatives to this commitment. For the moment, don't worry about whether they are good alternatives; just put down whatever has crossed your mind. What have you considered doing instead of this commitment? Exercise example:

- Quit working out altogether. Embrace a low-energy lifestyle.
- Try a totally different kind of exercise, like a team sport instead of a club workout.
- Walk every morning and call it good.
- Go drinking with friends instead.

Your turn: *What are your other choices? What alternatives to this commitment have crossed your mind?*

Take a moment to look at the list you just made. You may notice that one or more options are fairly good ideas. You may also notice options that are ridiculous and don't reflect what you want. Let's start with items on the list that have potential. Which of them, if any, could be a good choice for actualizing your commitment? For example, on the exerciser's list:

- Joining a team might be a good alternative.
- Taking a walk some mornings might be a good choice too (especially with that new music in the headphones).

Notice these are simply different ways of investing in the same goal—regular exercise.

Your turn: *Is there anything on your list that could do a good job of actualizing your commitment? If not, that's okay. If so, great.*

Now identify the items on the list that don't reflect your desired commitment. Identify the choices—concrete or imaginary—that pull your attention away, the ones that might seem attractive in the moment but don't help with your long-term goals. Think about how you can give that choice less attention or devalue it when it comes up. For example, our exerciser might pick the item that says, "Go drinking with friends instead," and she might develop the following plan to ignore that choice:

- I can tell my friends I am never available on Monday, Wednesday, and Friday evenings so they won't even ask.
- I can change the screen saver on my computer so I'm not constantly looking at a photo of the gang at the corner bar.
- I can see if any of my friends want to exercise with me instead of going to happy hour.

Your turn: *What steps can you take to ignore or devalue your other choices?*

Congratulations on Going All In!

Committing to what you want used to be a mystery; it seemed like a matter of will, something you "just do." Now you know there are four specific elements that predict your level of commitment, and some of those elements are within your control. Instead of trying to will yourself to be committed, you can reflect on your treasures, troubles, contributions, and choices and take concrete steps to increase the likelihood of your success. You won't be able to control everything, and sometimes you'll have to make tough choices. But when you're aware of these factors and you influence them as much as you can, your commitment will be both clarified and strengthened.

Additional Resources

I recommend the following books to further your goals. While they don't discuss commitment specifically, they each address the commitment elements in a unique and thoughtful way.

The How of Happiness: A New Approach to Getting the Life You Want
Sonja Lyubomirsky (Penguin Books, 2008)

This book is about generating greater happiness from the inside; it is also about how to *treasure* what you have. Based on the author's years of scientific research, it helps readers apply the lessons through quizzes and exercises.

Crucial Conversations: Tools for Talking When Stakes Are High
Kerry Patterson, Joseph Grenny, Ron McMillan, and Al
   Switzler (McGraw-Hill, 2011)

This is a great resource for talking about *troubles*. Based on the authors' observations of high performers, this book spells out how to talk about difficult and important topics at work and in relationships.

*The 7 Habits of Highly Effective People: Powerful Lessons in
   Personal Change*
Stephen R. Covey (Free Press, 2004)

This book was originally published in 1990. If you've never read it, or if it's been a while, pick up a copy. The author does an excellent job of motivating readers to identify and *contribute* to the most important areas of their lives.

The Paradox of Choice: Why More Is Less
Barry Schwartz (Harper Perennial, 2005)

This author makes the following claim and supports it well: As much as we like to have choices, too many choices can be a disadvantage. Schwartz is one of the developers of the original maximization scale, so he offers a lot of relevant research on the downside of choices.

I also recommend this online resource for committing to a goal: www.stickk.com.

Created by economics professors at Yale, stickK helps you stay with a goal by using the side bet principle. You tell stickK what you want to be committed to, such as spending a certain number of hours working out or studying, and then you input the financial penalty you will incur if you don't follow through, such as sending a hundred dollars to a political party you don't like. In addition, you publicly declare your commitment and allow others to track your progress.

All In
Action Plan Steps in Summary

- What do you want to be more committed to, and why?
- What do you currently treasure about your commitment, including the big and small?
- What new treasures could you add to the equation? What could you do differently, or what could you ask for, large and small?
- What step will you take to begin creating each treasure, and by when?
- Write a letter to your future self. Include the treasures you have as a result of this commitment. Write as though it's already happened and you are feeling great about following though with your commitment.
- What are the troubles of this commitment, including the big and small?
- Which of these are acceptable troubles, and which are troubles you'd like to change?
- What could you do to ease each trouble? This is the brainstorming phase, so include whatever comes to you, no limits. What could you do, or what could you ask for?
- What one or two solutions are you willing to try? Include any steps, with deadlines.
- What have you already put into this commitment in terms of time, talent, tenderness, and/or tangibles?

Commit to Win

- What new contributions can you make in terms of time, talent, tenderness, and/or tangibles? Or what kind of side bet can you create?

- Which of your ideas are you going to do right away, and by when?

- What are your other choices? What alternatives to this commitment have crossed your mind?

- Might any of these alternatives do a good job of actualizing your commitment?

- What steps can you take to ignore or devalue your other choices?

CHAPTER 8

Moving On

Tʜɪs chapter outlines the action plan to help you with moving on. Perhaps it's time to admit your current business plan isn't working or you're with a partner who isn't right for you long term. Maybe you feel stuck serving on a committee, or going out with friends who always bring you down. You might feel guilty about your desire to move on. You may also realize the only way to bring new and more meaningful commitments into your life is to let go of what doesn't work.

While it's difficult to "will" yourself to be less committed, there are ways of thinking and acting that allow your attachment to naturally decline. Specifically, this occurs when you put less emphasis on treasures and contributions, become clear about troubles, and perhaps most important, identify your choices. For this action plan you'll see an example of someone who wants to reduce her commitment to a romantic relationship, but your action plan will look different because you and your situation are unique.

Step One: Define Your De-commitment

First, identify the area where you wish to be less committed, as well as the reason. Be as specific as possible. I'll show an example first, and then it's your turn. Remember to have pen and paper handy.

- The What: I want to reduce my commitment to my boyfriend.
- The Why: I know this is a temporary relationship (he's not marriage material), and the longer I stay in it, the harder it will be to leave.

Now it's your turn: *What do you want to be less committed to and why?*

Step Two: Think Differently About Treasures

What are the main things about this relationship, job, or activity you treasure? It might seem strange to focus on treasures since you are wanting to let go, but this is an important step; you'll see why in a minute. For now, list the aspects of this commitment that are *currently* rewarding, and not the things that you received in the past or are hoping for in the future. The more specific you are at this stage, the easier it will be to generate action steps. For example, our dater might list the following treasures:

- The companionship/not being alone.
- The laughter and humor.
- The opportunity to travel.

Your turn: *What do you currently treasure about this commitment? What is rewarding to you?*

Now add to the list any treasures you used to receive but don't anymore. Also add the treasures you've been hoping will appear in the future. Again, be as specific as you can. In our relationship example, she might write:

- We used to laugh a lot more than we do now; I've been hoping for more of that again.
- I have been hoping for (and asking for) nonsexual, comforting touch and affection.
- I have been hoping to be treated more respectfully, especially in front of other people.

Your turn: *What future treasures have you been hoping for? What returning treasures have you been hoping for?*

Step Three: Reframing Treasures

Now for the exciting part, the step where you see that this person, job, or activity doesn't "own" these treasures—they can be found in other places if you begin to look and think creatively. Here you'll brainstorm where else you could gain the treasures from your two lists. At this point, don't worry about whether you *want* to get the treasures somewhere else. This brainstorm is to show that you have options; whether or not you take them is up to you. Our girlfriend might list the following as other ways to experience what she treasures:

- I could experience companionship and feeling respected with like-minded coworkers.

- I could get affection from my dog, who loves to cuddle.
- I could experience traveling with a tour group, or taking a language class.

Your turn: *Identify at least one other way you could experience each treasure you listed.*

Which of those options are you willing to get started on right now? Select one or more from your list and identify an action step that would move you toward that option, along with when you will complete that step. Each time you make a new choice, you become less dependent on your current commitment. Here are some examples from our dater:

- I will join my coworkers for lunch instead of talking to my boyfriend on the phone, starting tomorrow.
- I will give my dog a bath on Wednesday.
- I will try out the Spanish class offered by the extended learning program that starts in three weeks.

Your turn: *What steps can you take to create these treasures elsewhere, and by when will you take those steps?*

Step Four: Thinking Differently About Troubles

If you are thinking of getting out of this situation, the troubles associated with it are probably quite clear in your mind. Here you will list them. Be sure to include the troubling aspects that aren't necessarily anyone's "fault," but that reflect a mismatch between you and this activity or person. You might even include the troubles in which you play a role. In a moment you'll use this list to identify which of the problems are changeable and which are perpetual. Once again, be as specific as you can, as you'll see in this example troubles list:

- I have been less active with my friends because of how much time he wants to spend together. I'm feeling isolated.
- He makes fun of my clothes. It might just be his sense of humor, but it feels controlling.
- I get embarrassed by the comments he makes about me around other people.
- I'm not feeling like the passionate, alive, free person I used to be.

Your turn: *What are the troubles you are experiencing in this commitment?*

For each trouble you listed, note how long it has existed and your previous attempts to fix it, if any. Here's one example from our dater's list:

Embarrassing comments around other people

- This has occurred since day one, so 14 months.
- I've tried talking to him about the things he says when we are out, I've tried laughing them off, I've tried explaining him to people, and ultimately I've given up and am more comfortable when we just stay in.

Your turn: *How long has the trouble existed and what previous attempts, if any, have you made to fix it?*

Given your description, do you think the majority of these

troubles are changeable or perpetual? In other words, are they fixable or are they permanent? If you aren't sure, consider how long you'd be willing to keep trying. Take a minute to note your answers. Here's an example from our dater:

> Since these troubles have occurred for much of our relationship and nothing I have done has made a difference, my best guess is that they are perpetual. I'm still willing to try a little longer. Two months at most.

Your turn: *Are the majority of these troubles changeable or perpetual? How long are you willing to keep trying?*

If you think the troubles might be changeable and/or you want to give it a little more time, what one or two things are you willing to try as a last-ditch effort? Is there anything else you'd like to attempt before reducing your commitment? This step is not necessary—if you're ready, you're ready!—but if you have one last idea to potentially turn things around, write it down. From our example:

> The last thing I will try is letting him know we have two months to work on these things before I call it quits.

Your turn: *What other steps, if any, would you like to try before moving forward and reducing your commitment?*

As you look at the inventories you've written, you may notice there are as many troubles as treasures. Remember that to feel satisfied with a commitment, you need about five times as many positives (treasures) as negatives (troubles). If the current ratio is not acceptable and doesn't seem likely to change, it's time to consider reducing your contributions and identifying your choices. That's where we're headed next.

Step Five: Decreasing Contributions

One of the reasons you're likely still in this commitment is because of how much you have contributed to it. When you give a lot of yourself and your resources, it becomes increasingly difficult to change course. So in this step, you'll make a plan to reduce your contributions.

To begin, list the contributions you have made to this commitment. In what ways have you given your time, talent, tenderness, and/or tangibles? What financial or emotional investments have you made? Example from our dater:

- Being with him for 14 months.
- "Loaning" him $1,200 to fix his car.
- Telling people I love him and everything is good.
- Going on trips—photos and shared memories.

Your turn: *What contributions have you made to this commitment?*

As you look at your list, please acknowledge and congratulate yourself for all you've given. You have shown you are able to deeply invest in things that are important to you. Now that you want to move on, however, it's time to decrease those contributions.

Where could you pull back on contributing your time, talent, tenderness, and/or tangibles? Where and how can you stop investing yourself in this commitment? Be specific if you can. In our example:

- I can mentally "write off" the $1,200. More important, I can avoid loaning him more money in the future.

- I can tell some trusted people that I'm actually not happy and I'm thinking of leaving.
- I can avoid planning another trip with him.
- I can stop wearing his sweatshirt around the house.

Your turn: *Where and how can you stop investing yourself in this commitment?*

Step Six: Maximizing Choices

Now for the most important part of decreasing attachment: seeing you have other choices. You may have been living with the limited belief that you don't have any other options. You do. You just have to brainstorm what they are and start taking steps to explore the possibilities.

In this step make a list of your alternatives to this commitment. Where else could you get some of the benefits of this job, relationship, or activity? Use your imagination to think of the concrete alternatives you could create. Don't hold anything back—even ideas that seem silly can lead to creative (and realistic) options. Our dater might list the following alternatives to being in this relationship:

- I could make friendships my main relationship for now.
- I could focus on my career and get out of dating for a while.
- I could have coffee with the new client who asked me out.
- I could join the Peace Corps.
- I could check out a dating website.

Your turn: *What are your options?*

Now it's time to develop action steps that bring you closer to the most appealing choice. If one particular option stands out, create a comprehensive list of steps you can take to move toward it. If there are several choices you find potentially appealing, write down the initial "feeler" step you'd need to take for each. Taking feeler steps will help you to find your most attractive option. Depending on your situation, this may be a simple process, or it may require some contemplation and research. If you're ready to give yourself a deadline, write that down too. Example:

- Make friendships my main relationship for now: If I want to stay put and give myself some time to think it over before I make the decision to leave him, this is a good option. Steps I could begin now are:

  > Send out e-mails to people I haven't seen in a while and see who responds.
  >
  > Ask Quinn if she wants to go to a matinee for her birthday.
  >
  > Go to church again, starting this Sunday.

- Join the Peace Corps: This would give me the opportunity to travel (without him), to meet new people, and to get away from a relationship that has consumed me. The steps I could take to feel out this option are:

  > Go to the Peace Corps website to check out the requirements and procedure.
  >
  > Reconnect with old professors and employers who could serve as references.

> Talk to my uncles who have been in the Peace
> Corps about their experience.

Your turn: *What steps will bring you closer to your most appealing choices?*

Step Seven: Getting Support

Depending on the situation, you may benefit from support from a counselor, employer, spouse, coach, friend, or family member. For this final step, determine whom you will go to for support, and how each can assist you. Example:

- Mom can give me emotional support by phone day or night.
- Quinn can support me by doing fun activities with me.
- A counselor can give me professional assistance if leaving is harder than I think it will be.

Your turn: *Whom will you go to for support? How can they support you?*

Congratulations on Moving On!

You have shown you are capable of commitment. Now you get to choose where to put your energy and dedication next. By creating an action plan you've moved closer to creating new, more positive and meaningful commitments in your life.

Additional Resources

I recommend the following books to further your goals. They don't discuss commitment specifically, but each one provides perspectives and skills to help you determine new choices.

Too Good to Leave, Too Bad to Stay: A Step-by-Step Guide to Help You Decide Whether to Stay In or Get Out of Your Relationship
Mira Kirshenbaum (Penguin Group, 1997)

If you are trying to decide whether to stay with a relationship or let it go, this book offers helpful questions and solid advice based on the author's thirty-plus years as a psychotherapist. You'll also feel comforted to know you aren't the only person who's felt ambivalent and torn about a relationship.

Smart Choices: A Practical Guide to Making Better Decisions
John S. Hammond, Ralph L. Keeney, and Howard Raiffa (Crown Business, 2002)

Getting out of a commitment means leaving a past decision and making a new one. This book provides a series of steps for making good decisions in both personal and professional contexts.

The Dip: A Little Book That Teaches You When to Quit (and When to Stick)
Seth Godin (Penguin Group, 2007)

A little book (ninety-six pages) with a big idea: Sometimes it's okay to quit. This book focuses on the context of work and encourages readers to stick with what they're best at (the right stuff) and let the rest go (the wrong stuff).

When I Say No, I Feel Guilty
Manuel J. Smith (Bantam, 1985)

When you want to remove yourself from commitments that involve other people (such as neighbors, friends, and lovers), you need to have the ability to say no. If this is something you could work on, check out this now-classic book that can help you step into your assertive self.

This online resource is also helpful, if you are thinking about ending a relationship:

35 Questions and Thoughts Before You Say, "It's Over"
Rita Watson, *Psychology Today*, 2013
http://www.psychologytoday.com/blog/love-and-
     gratitude/201301/35-questions-and-thoughts-you-say-
     its-over

Moving On
Action Plan Steps in Summary

- What do you want to be less committed to and why?
- What do you currently treasure about this commitment? What is rewarding to you?
- What future treasures have you been hoping for? What returning treasures have you been hoping for?

- For each treasure, identify at least one other way you could experience that treasure.

- What steps can you take to create these treasures elsewhere, and by when will you take those steps?

- What are the troubles you are experiencing in this commitment?

- How long has the trouble existed and what previous attempts, if any, have you made to fix it?

- Are the majority of these troubles changeable or perpetual? How long are you willing to keep trying?

- What other steps, if any, would you like to try before moving forward and reducing your commitment?

- What contributions have you made to this commitment?

- Where and how can you stop investing yourself in this commitment?

- What are your options?

- What steps will take you closer to your most appealing choices?

- Whom will you go to for support? How can they support you?

■ CHAPTER 9 ■

Assisting Others

THE purpose of this chapter is to create an action plan that helps you assist others to greater commitment. Perhaps you want to ensure you're doing all you can to encourage commitment among your employees or clients, or within a personal relationship. While you can't make anyone commit, people are generally more committed when they have higher levels of treasures and contributions, and lower levels of troubles and choices. You'll notice there are a lot of elements to this action plan. If it's too much to do all at once, begin with one or two steps and work through the chapter slowly. Throughout these pages you'll see an example of a volunteer coordinator who wants to encourage greater commitment from his volunteer team. Your action plan will look different based on the unique elements of your situation.

Step One: Define the Commitment

Whom do you wish to be more committed? What do you want them to be committed to and why? Identify the purpose of encouraging greater commitment in this situation. As with the other lists of action steps, the more specific you can be, the better. I'll show an example first and then it's your turn.

- The Who: The ten people who are currently signed up as ongoing volunteers.
- The What: I want them to be more devoted to our non-profit. I want them to keep their names on the "regulars" list, and work as many events as possible.
- The Why: With a consistent group we get in a groove and the work becomes more efficient and fun. Most of all, this campaign helps a lot of people and we can't make it happen without our volunteers.

Now it's your turn: *In whom do you want to encourage commitment? What do you want them to be committed to, and why?*

Step Two: Identify and Increase Treasures

Now create an inventory of the things about this commitment that the other person or people likely treasure. What rewards do they receive from being involved? If you aren't sure off the top of your head, observe, listen, and ask questions. It's helpful to get good data here because when you know what they treasure, you can maintain or increase those benefits. Let's start with an example from our volunteer coordinator. He might note that his volunteer group treasures the following:

- Knowing they are making a difference.
- Developing relationships with like-minded people.
- Fun awards at the end of events.

Now it's your turn: *What treasures does the other person(s) experience in this commitment?*

Of the treasures you've just listed, identify a few you could increase or emphasize. This is an opportunity to play to your strengths. If something is a benefit to others, expand and highlight it. Our coordinator might write:

- I can emphasize the feeling they are making a difference by reading thank-you notes from those we serve at the beginning of meetings.
- I can increase relationships with like-minded people by hosting social gatherings in addition to work gatherings.
- I can increase the fun of awards by adding a surprise or "random" award that no one expects.

Now it's your turn: *What are a few treasures you could increase or emphasize? How could you strengthen these benefits?*

Next, consider new treasures that could be added. What do you think the other person or people value that they aren't currently getting? Again, this may require some research. Listen to them, ask questions, and think about the previous feedback you've received. For extrinsic treasures, consider if you could offer something unique or random (see the beginning of Chapter 3 for a refresher). For intrinsic treasures in a work situation, recall that key treasures include things like task importance and enjoying the process. In relationships, intrinsic treasures are subjective, so it's important to consider the other person's perspective. Examples from the volunteer team:

NEW TREASURE: COMPLEXITY

Sometimes I tell them what to do and exactly how to do it, like when we make the posters. Next time I can let them know the outcome needed, but allow them to be creative about how to get there.

NEW TREASURE: HUMOR

I think they would enjoy the process more if I brought some humor to the situation. It always feels a little serious, and I've gotten feedback that folks would value some levity. Maybe I could have a funny hat day, or bring your best (non-offensive) joke day, or play some fun music while we stuff those envelopes. I could even have a movie on while we work, like *Groundhog Day* or *Caddyshack*.

Now it's your turn: *What new treasures could you add?*

Next you'll create a specific plan. Look at the items you've just listed, and identify a new treasure you'd like your person or people to have. Write out what you will do and by when to begin creating that treasure. Be specific. For example:

New Treasure: Complexity

The next group project is in three weeks. For that project, I'm going to let them know the end goal, and then get out of their way and allow for the creative process.

New Treasure: Humor

Make sure I know how to work the tech equipment (this afternoon), and rent *Groundhog Day* via Netflix (for delivery next Tuesday).

Step Three: Identify Troubles

This next step isn't necessarily fun, but it is important. Here you'll identify the downsides of this commitment for the person or people involved. No matter how great a relationship, job, or activity is, there are always costs. If you can be honest about what the troubles are for the other(s) then you can consider how to minimize them. So, what is likely troubling to the person or people? Think of the big troubles, and also think of the subtle things that are annoying or difficult. As an example, our coordinator acknowledges the following troubles might decrease his team's commitment to the monthly meetings:

- Lots of complaints about the time of our meetings—7 a.m.
- Complaints that the chairs are uncomfortable, "rickety," etc.
- Comments that Jessica takes up the majority of talk time.

Now it's your turn: *What are troubles for your person or people? Be as specific as you can.*

Step Four: Decrease Troubles

For each trouble you listed, consider ways you could lessen it. This is the brainstorming phase. If you can't think of anything that will improve a particular trouble, that's okay; there are many other parts of the equation you can focus on. But don't sell yourself short. Most troubles can at least be minimized. Think of actions you could take yourself, and also think of ways you could get outside help. For example:

- Early 7 a.m. meetings

    Tell my manager there have been complaints about 7 a.m., and see if we can move it to 8 a.m. Even 7:30 would help because people would see I'm trying to make it better.

    Get in extra early myself to make sure the coffee is ready.

- Uncomfortable, rickety chairs

    Ask my manager to replace the three bad chairs. I think it's only three—it just seems like more when you're the one in the chair.

    Bring in a few decent chairs from my office waiting area.

    Put a label on the bad chairs along with a candy bar so people might actually want to pick them and then feel better about it!

- Jessica taking the majority of talk time

  Ask our trainer for some suggestions on how he keeps individuals from taking over. It seems like he does a few things that help with that.

  Go around the room and allow each person some time to offer suggestions (rather than a free-for-all).

  Give Jessica a task during the meeting, like taking the minutes, so she is partially occupied.

Now it's your turn: *What could you do to ease each trouble? This is the brainstorming phase, so put down whatever comes to you. What could you do, or how could you get help?*

Which of the solutions you've listed do you think might work? Note the solutions you are willing to try, along with a deadline. If the solution has several steps, identify each step with deadlines. For example:

- Monday, I will e-mail my manager and ask for an appointment to discuss the time of the morning meeting, and the cost of replacing the chairs.
- By next Thursday's meeting, I will make the signs and buy the candy bars.
- Today, I will e-mail the trainer and ask for an appointment to discuss strategies for dealing with Jessica.

Your turn: *What solutions are you willing to try? Include any steps, with deadlines.*

Step Five: Acknowledge Contributions

This next step is to gauge their current level of investment. What contributions have they made so far? List the things they have already put into this commitment. Think of all four categories: time (days, years, energy), talent (skills, creativity), tenderness (sharing themselves, emotional investment), and tangibles (money, material items). Remember, contributions are nearly synonymous with commitment, so you want a good, realistic gauge here. Our coordinator's inventory might read:

- All of them signed up to be ongoing volunteer staff.
- Most "liked" our Facebook page and make comments now and then.
- Many have invited their friends to the one-day events.
- Many have shown they are emotionally invested in the people we serve.
- Half the group has been with us for over two years.
- All completed the certification training.

Your turn: *What has your person or people already put into this commitment in terms of time, talent, tenderness, and/or tangibles?*

As you look at this list, you may notice that in many ways the commitment is already a part of them. Allow yourself to acknowledge what they have given. When the time is right, acknowledge *them* for what they have given.

Step Six: Increase Contributions

The more they invest, the more committed they are likely to be. Therefore, brainstorm some new ways you could get them to contribute. What are some simple ways you could encourage them to increase their investment? Remember, the more specific, the more helpful, like in this example:

- Have *them* pick the comedy movies to play while we stuff envelopes.
- Run a Facebook contest to see who can get the most new people to "like" us.
- Let them decide what will go on this year's T-shirt.

Your turn: *What contributions could you invite your person or people to make in terms of time, talent, tenderness, and/or tangibles?*

Of your ideas, select one or more you are willing to do right away, and give yourself a deadline. For example:

> For the Facebook contest, I will select a prize this weekend. By the following Friday, I will write up the rules and post.

Your turn: *Which of your ideas are you going to do right away, and by when?*

Step Seven: Acknowledge Choices

Remember that commitment is impacted by whether people perceive other good choices. Write a quick inventory of the options they likely see. What choices do they have besides being committed to you or your goal? Our coordinator's inventory might read:

- They could volunteer for one of the other well-coordinated nonprofits, like Habitat for Humanity.
- They could volunteer for a onetime event with us or someone else, rather than an ongoing commitment.
- They could spend their time with a private enterprise, like their church or synagogue.

Your turn: *What choices does your person or people have besides being committed to you or your goal?*

Step Eight: Stand out Among Choices

While it's tempting to announce that you are better than their other choices and they shouldn't look elsewhere, that doesn't tend to be effective. As discussed in Chapter 6, telling others not to look at their alternatives can backfire and actually increase their attraction to those other options. A better approach is to determine what you have that the other choices don't, and then feature that strength.

So, what differentiates you from other options? What do you have or could you have that others don't? Freewrite a few sentences and see what comes to you. It's okay to acknowledge your strengths! From our coordinator:

We're different because of the ongoing nature of what we
do. You don't show up one time and meet a bunch of

people you'll never see again. There is a real chance for community here.

Your turn: *What differentiates you from the person or people's other options?*

How can you communicate or show what makes you different from the other choices? What can you do to highlight how you or your group is unique? Example:

Emphasizing the "community" difference:

- Develop a group web page where they can exchange information with each other and stay connected between meetings.
- Spend time at each monthly meeting doing an activity that helps us learn about each other on a personal level. (There will be time for this once Jessica isn't taking up most of the talk time.)
- Use the phrase "community of volunteers" in our marketing materials.

Your turn: *How can you communicate or show what it is that makes you different from other choices without drawing attention to these choices or putting them down?*

Congratulations on Assisting Others!

Now you have a plan going forward, a way to create an environment in which treasures are maximized, troubles are minimized, contributions are invited, and other choices seem less attractive.

While you can't force anyone to be committed, you know what to do to increase your odds. The people who were meant to join you will, and they'll be more satisfied and dedicated in the long run.

Additional Resources

The following books are excellent resources for creating an environment in which high levels of commitment are more likely. Each one discusses ways to increase treasures and decrease troubles at home or at work.

Drive: The Surprising Truth About What Motivates Us
Daniel Pink (Riverhead Books, 2011)

This is a great book about the science of motivation. It details why intrinsic rewards are essential for high-performance (and enjoyment) at work.

The Seven Principles for Making Marriage Work
John Gottman and Nan Silver (Harmony, 2000)

This book explains the common troubles that are associated with an increased risk for divorce. The authors show how to create a successful and emotionally intelligent relationship based on the lead author's decades of scientific research. Also included are helpful quizzes, and exercises to do with your partner.

Getting to Yes: Negotiating Agreement Without Giving In
Roger Fisher, William L. Ury, and Bruce Patton (Penguin
    Books, 2011)

Another classic. Originally published almost thirty years ago, it's still the gold standard in negotiating with others to meet important goals while maintaining relationships. This book emerges from research from the Harvard Negotiation Project.

The Five Love Languages: How to Express Heartfelt Commitment to Your Mate
Gary Chapman (Northfield Publishing, 2009)

Chapman's book explains how people in relationships have different ways of understanding that they are loved. To create a bond your partner will treasure, it's helpful to know their "love language." Many people have found this book useful in their relationships.

Assisting Others
Action Plan Steps in Summary

- In whom do you want to encourage commitment? What do you want them to be committed to, and why?

- What treasures does the other person(s) experience in this commitment?

- What are a few treasures you could increase or emphasize? How could you strengthen the benefits the person or people already receive?

- What new treasures could you add?

- What is a trouble to your person or people? Be as specific as you can.

- What could you do to ease each trouble? This is the brainstorming phase, so include whatever comes to you. What could you do, or how could you get help?

- What solutions are you willing to try? Include any steps, with deadlines.

Commit to Win

- What has the person or people already put into this commitment in terms of time, talent, tenderness, and/or tangibles?

- What contributions could you invite them to make in terms of time, talent, tenderness, and/or tangibles?

- Which of your ideas are you going to do right away, and by when?

- What choices does your person or people have besides being committed to you or your goal?

- What differentiates you from their other options?

- How can you communicate or show what it is that makes you different from the other choices without drawing attention to those choices or putting them down?

ACKNOWLEDGMENTS

I once heard a quotation: "If I had it to do all over again, I'd get help." I'm happy to say that in the writing of this book, I got help. I couldn't have completed this work without the support of so many people, from my family and colleagues to the publishing team. I'm beyond grateful to my husband, Jeff Stipp, for dealing with me during the intense time of research and writing. He picked up the slack around the house, served as my emotional counselor, and read every word I wrote, improving on many of them. Thank you to my mom, Jesse Reeder, who read the "ugly drafts." At that point they were chapters only a mother could love, but she provided encouragement and suggestions to get the writing ready for someone outside the family.

Thank you to the social scientists, writers, and friends who read and commented on chapters in various stages of doneness: Mary Pritchard, Shannon Kolakowski, Darren George, and Kristine Bingham, I am so grateful for your enthusiasm and talent. I also appreciate those who allowed me to interview them for this book. Your stories and experiences made the data meaningful.

I am indebted to the publishing team. I am lucky to have Laurie Abkemeier from DeFiore and Company as my agent. Laurie knows the publishing industry inside and out and was perfect for me as a first-time author. I'm similarly grateful to the whole team at Hudson Street Press, particularly Brittney Ross, my insightful, smart, patient, and encouraging editor. A special thanks to Meghan Stevenson, who identified my proposal as worthy of becoming a book.

I am grateful to my family and friends, and to the administration at Boise State University for seeing value in this project. Many thanks to: Alan Reeder, Travis Reeder, Melissa Lavitt, Rick Moore, Christine Moore, Kasha Glynn, and Tabbi Simenc. Perhaps most of all, thank you to my past and present students. I treasure your support and enthusiasm.

NOTES

Chapter 1: A Fresh Look at Commitment

6   *dedication* **and** *constraint***:** See, for example: Stanley, S. M., & Markman, H. J. (1992). Assessing commitment in personal relationships. *Journal of Marriage and the Family, 54*(3), 595–608.

7   **Consider Holly, a four-year-old tortoiseshell-colored cat:** KSBW.com (2013, January 8). *Lost cat makes incredible 190-mile journey home.* Retrieved from http://www.ksbw.com/news/Lost-cat-makes-incredible-190-mile-journey-home/-/1852/18053456/-/3ngx5dz/-/index.html.

9   **"A Strange Situation":** Ainsworth, M. D. S., & Bell, S. M. (1970). Attachment, exploration, and separation: Illustrated by the behavior of one-year-olds in a strange situation. *Child Development, 41*(1), 49–67.

11   **Some scholars argue that the commitment effect is a uniquely human and primate challenge:** See, for example, Arkes, H., & Ayton, P. (1999). The sunk cost and concorde effects: Are humans less rational than lower animals? *Psychological Bulletin, 125*(5), 591–600.

11   **even pigeons are susceptible to a form of the sunk cost fallacy:** See, for example: Macaskill, A., & Hackenberg, T. (2012). Providing a reinforcement history that reduces the sunk cost effect. *Behavioural Processes, 89*(3), 212–218.

12   **Relationship researchers Leslie Baxter and Connie Bullis:** Baxter, L.,

& Bullis, C. (1986). Turning points in developing romantic relationships. *Human Communication Research, 12*(4), 469–493.

14 **Distinguished Yale psychologist Robert Sternberg:** Sternberg, R. J. (1988). *The triangle of love: Intimacy, passion, commitment.* New York: Basic Books.

20 **It's easy to think that if you are committed, you should see results right away:** The discussion of myths five and six was inspired by the first chapter of *Creating commitment: How to attract and retain talented employees by building relationships that last* (New York: Wiley, 2000), by Michael O'Malley.

Chapter 2: The Commitment Equation

30 **something tens of thousands of Americans are doing today to ease their financial burden:** Abbey, J. (2013, February 4). 5 tips for renting out your spare rooms [Video file]. Retrieved from http://abcnews.go .com/blogs/lifestyle/2013/02/5-tips-for-making-your-spare-rooms-rentable/.

31 **Formal cost-benefit analysis apparently began with talented road and bridge engineer:** The information in this section comes from: Ekelund, R. B., & Hébert, R. F. (1999). *Secret origins of modern microeconomics: Dupuit and the Engineers.* Chicago: University of Chicago Press.

33 **males slightly outnumbering females (one baby girl for every 1.05 baby boys):** Central Intelligence Agency. *The world factbook.* Retrieved from https://www.cia.gov/library/publications/the-world-factbook/fields/2018.html.

33 **the language we use to describe our interactions with others indicates a kind of exchange:** All information about Homans's ideas on exchange comes from his article: Homans, G. (1958). Social behavior as exchange. *American Journal of Sociology, 63*(6), 597–606.

35 **Blau offered a simple but significant equation for human interaction:** Blau, P. (1964). *Exchange and power in social life.* New York: Wiley.

37 **He called it *entrapment*:** Rubin, J. (1975). Conflict escalation and entrapment in international relations: A proposal. Research proposal.

37   **Sociologist Louis Kriesberg explained it like this:** Kriesberg, L. (2003). *Constructive conflicts: From escalation to resolution* (2nd ed.), p. 161. Lanham, MA: Rowman and Littlefield.

39   **formalized social exchange as a way of understanding how people develop and maintain relationships:** Kelley, H., & Thibaut, J. (1978). *Interpersonal relations: A theory of interdependence.* New York: Wiley.

40   **Rusbult published a framework called the Investment Model:** Rusbult, C. E. (1980). Commitment and satisfaction in romantic associations: A test of the investment model. *Journal of Experimental Social Psychology, 16,* 172–186.

41   **A meta-analysis of these studies showed that, statistically, these variables accounted for almost two-thirds of a person's decision to commit:** Le, B., & Agnew, C. R. (2003). Commitment and its theorized determinants: A meta-analysis of the Investment Model. *Personal Relationships, 10*(1), 37–57. (A meta-analysis is a statistical method of systematically combining the results from multiple research studies on a similar topic to discover patterns and places of agreement and disagreement.)

Chapter 3: Treasures: What Do You Value?

52   **your level of commitment to an organization is fairly static:** See, for example: Mowday, R., Steers, R., & Porter, L. (1982). *Employee-organization linkages: The psychology of commitment, absenteeism, and turnover.* New York: Academic Press.

52   **Because organizational commitment predicts both employee effort and turnover:** Mathieu, J. E., & Zajac, D. M. (1990). A review and meta-analysis of the antecedents, correlates, and consequences of organizational commitment. *Psychological Bulletin, 108*(2), 171–194.

52   **Sadly, record numbers of us currently want to quit our jobs:** Weisul, K. (2011, December 2). *84 percent of workers looking to leave their jobs.* Retrieved from http://www.cbsnews.com/8301-505125_162-57335303/84-percent-of-workers-looking-to-leave-their-jobs/.

52   **three intrinsic treasures are associated with greater organizational commitment:** Joo, B. K., & Lim, T. (2009). The effects of organizational

learning culture, perceived job complexity, and proactive personality on organizational commitment and intrinsic motivation. *Journal of Leadership and Organizational Studies, 16*(1), 48–60.

54 **According to the studies documented in Daniel Pink's *Drive*:** Pink, D. (2011). *Drive: The surprising truth about what motivates us.* New York: Riverhead Trade.

55 **All told, most people who begin a fitness program stop:** Kolata, G. (2012, June 18). Sold on the feeling, if not the benefits to health. *New York Times.*

55 **Researchers in Greece:** Alexandris, K., Zahariadis, P., Tsorbatzoudis, C., & Grouios, G. (2002). Testing the sport commitment model in the context of exercise and fitness participation. *Journal of Sport Behavior, 25*(3), 217.

56 **A 2012 *New York Times* article questioned the strategy:** Kolata. Sold on the feeling.

56 **Take all those young competitive soccer players in Spain:** Garcia-Mas, A., Palou, P., Gili, M., Ponseti, X., Borras, P. A., Vidal, J., . . . Sousa, C. (2010). Commitment, enjoyment and motivation in young soccer competitive players. *Spanish Journal of Psychology, 13*(2), 609–616.

56 **In fact, a study of U.S. youth in a variety of competitive sports:** Zahariadis, P., Tsorbatzoudis, H., & Alexandris, K. (2006). Self-determination in sport commitment. *Perceptual and Motor Skills, 102*(2), 405–420.

59 **Some relationships are what you might call *tit-for-tat* relationships:** The term *tit for tat* was coined by professors Anatol Rapoport and Robert Axelrod. You can read about it in many of Axelrod's writings; for example: Axelrod, R., & Hamilton, W. (1981). The evolution of cooperation. *Science, 211*(4489), 1390–1396.

59 **Social scientists call this a *communal* relationship:** The contrast between the two types of relationships discussed here was first introduced by: Clark, M., & Mills, J. (1979). Interpersonal attraction in exchange and communal relationships. *Journal of Personality and Social Psychology, 37*(1), 12–24.

60 **we experience a kind of cognitive overlap between us and our partner:** Agnew, C. R., Van Lange, P. A. M., Rusbult, C. E., & Langston, C.

A. (1998). Cognitive interdependence: Commitment and the mental representation of close relationships. *Journal of Personality and Social Psychology, 74*(4), 939–954.

60 **You can also use communal language:** Ibid.

62 **This situation may sound absurd, but it was the setup of an inventive researcher:** Greenberg, J. (1988). Equity and workplace status: A field experiment. *Journal of Applied Psychology, 73*(4), 606–613.

64 **research supports this very chain of events:** Hendrix, W. H., Robbins, T., Miller, J., & Summers, T. P. (1998). Effects of procedural and distributive justice on factors predictive of turnover. *Journal of Social Behavior and Personality, 13*(4), 611–632.

65 **Take the classic 1973 study:** Berscheid, E., Walster, E., & Bohrnstedt, G. (1973, November). The happy American body: A survey report. *Psychology Today, 7*, 119–131.

66 **Couples go through periods of imbalance like this all the time and stay intact:** In fact, when married couples are asked how much they each contributed to a specific household task, invariably both people will claim they contributed more. See, for example: Ross, M., & Sicoly, F. (1979). Egocentric biases in availability and attribution. *Journal of Personality and Social Psychology, 37*(3), 322–336.

67 **Social psychology researcher Susan Sprecher tracked one hundred couples over five years:** Sprecher, S. (2001). Equity and social exchange in dating couples: Associations with satisfaction, commitment, and stability. *Journal of Marriage and Family, 63*(3), 599–613.

70 **Some community clinics have experimented with randomly rewarding their outpatients:** Petry, N., Weinstock, J., & Alessi, S. (2011). A randomized trial of contingency management delivered in the context of group counseling. *Journal of Consulting and Clinical Psychology, 79*(5), 686–696.

71 **You can do something creative, like naming a food item in the cafeteria after them:** These ideas were inspired by: Glanz, B. (1993). *The creative communicator: 399 ways to make your business communications meaningful and inspiring.* New York: McGraw-Hill.

72 **This appears to be an acute risk in abusive partnerships:** Dutton,

D., & Painter, S. (1993). Emotional attachments in abusive relationships: A test of traumatic bonding theory. *Violence and Victims, 8*(2),
105–120.

72 **The hostage develops a bond with her perpetrator:** Fabrique, N., Ro-
mano, S., Vecchi, G., & Van Hasselt, V. (2007). Understanding Stockholm Syndrome. *FBI Law Enforcement Bulletin, 76*(7).

73 **Their company has long used energy-efficient technology:** http://
www.benjerry.com/company/sear-reports/sear-2011.

74 **It's no wonder people employed by Ben and Jerry's feel good about
their work:** Dessler, G. (1993). *Winning commitment: How to build and
keep a competitive workforce.* New York: McGraw-Hill.

74 **This package, called Your Special Blend:** Starbucks.com (n.d.). *Working
at Starbucks.* Retrieved from http://www.starbucks.com/career-center/
working-at-starbucks.

76 **Gary Chapman's popular book, *The Five Love Languages*:** Chapman,
G. (2002). *The five love languages: How to express heartfelt commitment to
your mate.* Chicago: Northfield Publishing.

76 **Chapman's love languages have been tested by communication scholars and found to be valid:** Egbert, N., & Polk, D. (2006). Speaking the
language of relational maintenance: A validity test of Chapman's (1992)
five love languages. *Communication Research Reports, 23*(1), 19–26.

Chapter 4: Troubles: What's Holding You Back?

81 **It is estimated that nearly half of all Americans will drop out of their
church:** Roozen, D. (1980). Church dropouts: Changing patterns of
disengagement and re-entry. *Review of Religious Research, 21*(4), 427–
450. Note: Although this estimate is from 1980, a quick Google search
of "how many people quit church" will provide dozens of articles on the
increasing numbers of people leaving their churches across the nation.

87 **Eliza Byington was a PhD student at the University of Washington
Foster School of Business:** Churchman, P. (2009, April 28). *When you
work with a jerk: The bad apples study.* Retrieved from http://www.the
glasshammer.com/news/2009/04/28/when-you-work-with-a-jerk-the
-bad-apples-study/.

87 **Difficult people in the workplace have gone by many names:** Felps, W., Mitchell, T., & Byington, E. (2006). How, when, and why bad apples spoil the barrel: Negative group members and dysfunctional groups. *Research in Organizational Behavior, 27*, 175–222.

87 **On the National Public Radio show *This American Life*:** Will Felps described his dissertation in an interview with Ira Glass (2008). Ruining it for the rest of us, *This American Life*, episode 370.

89 **One group of authors, led by Roy Baumeister, of Florida State University:** Baumeister, R., Bratslavsky, E., Finkenauer, C., & Vohs, K. (2001). Bad is stronger than good. *Review of General Psychology, 5*(4), 323–370.

90 **A team of authors from the University of Pennsylvania agreed:** Rozin, P., & Royzman, E. B. (2001). Negativity bias, negativity dominance, and contagion. *Personality and Social Psychology Review, 5*(4), 296–320.

90 **Additionally, you must use cognitive effort to think optimistically about the negative event so it doesn't impact you more than necessary:** The cognitive effort explanation comes from: Taylor, S. (1991). Asymmetrical effects of positive and negative events: The mobilization-minimization hypothesis. *Psychological Bulletin, 110*(1), 67–85.

91 **that ending is what typically remains in our long-term memory:** Kahneman, D. (2011). *Thinking, fast and slow.* New York: Farrar, Straus and Giroux.

93 **Dawes and a colleague had just written an article titled "Linear Prediction of Marital Happiness":** Howard, J., & Dawes, R. (1976). Linear prediction of marital happiness. *Personality and Social Psychology Bulletin, 2*(4), 478–480.

94 **Gottman can predict whether a couple will stay together or divorce with over 90 percent accuracy:** The information on Gottman's research comes from two sources: 1) Gottman, J. (1996). Why marriages fail. In K. M. Galvin & P. J. Cooper (Eds.), *Making connections: Readings in relational communication.* Los Angeles: Roxbury. 2) Gottman, J., & Silver, N. (1999). *The seven principles for making marriage work.* New York: Three Rivers Press.

97 **Analyzing multiple reports over a ten-day-plus period, Miner found that the negative experiences influenced mood more than the positive**

ones: Miner, A., Glomb, T., & Hulin, C. (2005). Experience sampling mood and its correlates at work. *Journal of Occupational and Organizational Psychology, 78*(2), 171–195.

100 **according to the authors of the bestselling book *Crucial Conversations*:** Patterson, K. Grenny, J., McMillan, R., & Switzler, A. (2002). *Crucial conversations: Tools for talking when stakes are high.* New York: McGraw-Hill.

101 **In one study, they asked married people to think about a current marital problem and give their story for why the problem had occurred:** Fincham, F. D., & Bradbury, T. N. (1987). The impact of attributions in marriage: A longitudinal analysis. *Journal of Personality and Social Psychology, 53*(3), 510–517.

105 **They call these responses *loyalty, voice, neglect,* and *exit*:** The information on these four elements comes from two sources: 1) Rusbult, C., Johnson, D., & Morrow, G. (1986). Determinants and consequences of exit, voice, loyalty, and neglect: Responses to dissatisfaction in adult romantic involvements. *Human Relations, 39*(1), 45–63. 2) Rusbult, C., Farrell, D., Rogers, G., & Mainous III, A. (1988). Impact of exchange variables on exit, voice, loyalty, and neglect: An integrative model of responses to declining job satisfaction. *Academy of Management Journal, 31*(3), 599–627.

110 **The author of *The Gift of Fear*, Gavin de Becker:** de Becker, G. (1999). *The gift of fear.* New York: Random House Publishing Group.

111 **69 percent of marital issues are what he calls *perpetual problems*:** Gottman & Silver. *The seven principles for making marriage work.*

113 **seeing ourselves in the best light is essential to our happiness, well-being, and ability to persist in the face of setbacks:** Taylor, S., Collins, R., Skokan, L., & Aspinwall, L. (1989). Maintaining positive illusion in the face of negative information: Getting the facts without letting them get to you. *Journal of Social and Clinical Psychology, 8*(2), 114–129.

113 **Rusbult and her colleagues from the University of North Carolina:** Martz, J. M., Verette, J., Arriaga, X. B., Slovik, L. F., Cox, C. L., & Rusbult, C. E. (1998). Positive illusion in close relationships. *Personal Relationships, 5*, 159–181.

113 **Researchers from the University of Waterloo, in Ontario, Canada, had nearly two hundred couples complete questionnaires:** Murray, S., Holmes, J., & Griffin, D. (1996). The benefits of positive illusions: Idealization and the construction of satisfaction in close relationships. *Journal of Personality and Social Psychology, 70*(1), 79–98.

115 **The leading researcher in this area is Angela Duckworth:** The data on grit comes from: Duckworth, A. L., Peterson, C., Matthews, M. D., & Kelly, D. R. (2007). Grit: Perseverance and passion for long-term goals. *Journal of Personality and Social Psychology, 92*(6), 1087–1101.

Chapter 5: Contributions: How Much Have You Given?

125 **small initial commitments have a tendency to "grow their own legs":** Cialdini, R. (2007). *Influence: The psychology of persuasion.* New York: HarperCollins.

126 **people who were first invited to sign the petition were more likely to contribute:** Schwarzwald, J., Bizman, A., & Raz, M. (1983). The foot-in-the-door paradigm: Effects of second request size on donation probability and donor generosity. *Personality and Social Psychology Bulletin, 9*(3), 443–450.

129 **A team of researchers from Harvard, Princeton, and Duke wanted to find out:** Norton, M., Mochon, D., & Ariely, D. (2012). The IKEA Effect: When labor leads to love. *Journal of Consumer Psychology, 22*(3), 453–460.

133 **Jeffrey Rubin and Joel Brockner, psychologists from Tufts University:** Rubin, J. Z., & Brockner, J. (1975). Factors affecting entrapment in waiting situations: The Rosencrantz and Guildenstern effect. *Journal of Personality and Social Psychology, 31*(6), 1054–1063.

137 **Allan Teger, psychologist turned visual artist, calls *too-much-invested-to-quit*:** Teger, A. I., & Cary, M. (1980). *Too much invested to quit.* New York: Pergamon Press.

139 **Anne McCarthy and a research team from the Department of Management at Indiana University:** McCarthy, A. M., Schoorman, F. D., & Cooper, A. C. (1993). Reinvestment decisions by entrepreneurs: Ra-

tional decision-making or escalation of commitment? *Journal of Business Venturing, 8*(1), 9–24.

141 **A team of researchers from University of Denver's Center for Marital and Family Studies:** Stanley, S. M., Rhoades, G. K., & Markman, H. J. (2006). Sliding versus deciding: Inertia and the premarital cohabitation effect. *Family Relations, 55*(4), 499–509. For statistics, also see: Kline, G. H., Stanley, S. M., Markman, H. J., Olmos-Gallo, P. A., St. Peters, M., Whitton, S. W., & Prado, L. M. (2004). Timing is everything: Pre-engagement cohabitation and increased risk for poor marital outcomes. *Journal of Family Psychology, 18*(2), 311–318.

143 **The University of Denver team discovered that adding just *one* concrete investment:** Rhoades, G. K., Stanley, S. M., & Markman, H. J. (2010). Should I stay or should I go? Predicting dating relationship stability from four aspects of commitment. *Journal of Family Psychology, 24*(5), 543–550.

Chapter 6: Choices: What Are Your Alternatives?

155 **Nearly four hundred married people:** Osborn, J. L. (2012). When TV and marriage meet: A social exchange analysis of the impact of television viewing on marital satisfaction and commitment. *Mass Communication and Society, 15*(5), 739–757.

156 **Researchers at Florida State University:** Lambert, N. M., Negash, S., Stillman, T. F., Olmstead, S. B., & Fincham, F. D. (2012). A love that doesn't last: Pornography consumption and weakened commitment to one's romantic partner. *Journal of Social and Clinical Psychology, 31*(4), 410–438.

157 **What matters for commitment, according to the experiments of marketing researchers Kamal Gupta and David Stewart:** Gupta, K., & Stewart, D. W. (1996). Customer satisfaction and customer behavior: The differential role of brand and category expectations. *Marketing Letters, 7*(3), 249–263.

160 **Psychologist Rowland Miller invited people into the lab:** Miller, R. S. (1997). Inattentive and contented: Relationship commitment and atten-

tion to alternatives. *Journal of Personality and Social Psychology, 73*(4), 758–766.

161 **Actors have the highest unemployment rate:** *Wall Street Journal* analysis of Bureau of Labor Statistics data (2012). Unemployment rate by job. Retrieved from http://online.wsj.com/article/SB10001424052970203471004577145281015856726.html.

162 **This was the setup of a psychological study at the University of North Carolina:** Johnson, D. J., & Rusbult, C. E. (1989). Resisting temptation: Devaluation of alternative partners as a means of maintaining commitment in close relationships. *Journal of Personality and Social Psychology, 57*(6), 967–980.

163 **A team of researchers headed by C. Nathan DeWall:** DeWall, C. N., Maner, J. K., Deckman, T., & Rouby, D. A. (2011). Forbidden fruit: Inattention to attractive alternatives provokes implicit relationship reactance. *Journal of Personality and Social Psychology, 100*(4), 621–629.

164 **Consider how much you agree with these statements taken from the maximization scale:** Schwartz, B., Ward, A., Monterosso, J., Lyubomirsky, S., White, K., & Lehman, D. R. (2002). Maximizing versus satisficing: Happiness is a matter of choice. *Journal of Personality and Social Psychology, 83*(5), 1178–1197.

165 **Consider this example based on an experiment by Erin Sparks:** Sparks, E. A., Ehrlinger, J., & Eibach, R. P. (2012). Failing to commit: Maximizers avoid commitment in a way that contributes to reduced satisfaction. *Personality and Individual Differences, 52*(1), 72–77.

168 **Roughly 20 percent of the population:** Hazan, C., & Shaver, P. (1987). Romantic love conceptualized as an attachment process. *Journal of Personality and Social Psychology, 52*(3), 511–524.

169 **Indeed, study after study shows:** For a review of studies see: Birnie, C., Joy McClure, M., Lydon, J. E., & Holmberg, D. (2009). Attachment avoidance and commitment aversion: A script for relationship failure. *Personal Relationships, 16*(1), 79–97.

169 **Researchers from McGill University:** Ibid.

170 **psychologists from three universities showed that's what avoidant types tend to do:** DeWall, C. N., Lambert, N. M., Slotter, E. B., Pond

Jr., R. S., Deckman, T., Finkel, E. J., . . . Fincham, F. D. (2011). So far away from one's partner, yet so close to romantic alternatives: Avoidant attachment, interest in alternatives, and infidelity. *Journal of Personality and Social Psychology, 101*(6), 1302–1316.

171 **People with an avoidant attachment style report lower levels of commitment to their organizations as well:** The information in this paragraph comes from: Mikulincer, M., & Shaver, P. R. (2007). *Attachment in adulthood: Structure, dynamics, and change.* New York: Guilford Press.

INDEX

Index